GESTALTING ADDICTION: THE ADDICTION-FOCUSED GROUP THERAPY OF DR. RICHARD LOUIS MILLER

FRONTIERS IN PSYCHOTHERAPY SERIES
Edward Tick, *Series Editor*

GESTALTING ADDICTION:
THE ADDICTION-FOCUSED
GROUP THERAPY
OF
DR. RICHARD LOUIS MILLER

Angela Browne-Miller,
M.P.H., D.S.W., Ph.D.
Lecturer, School of Social Welfare
University of California at Berkeley

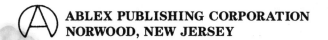
ABLEX PUBLISHING CORPORATION
NORWOOD, NEW JERSEY

Original illustrations including book cover by Angela Browne-Miller.

Copyright © 1993 by Ablex Publishing Corporation

Printed in the United States of America

Library of Congress Cataloging-in-Publication Data

Browne Miller, Angela, 1952-
   Gestalting addiction : the addiction-focused group therapy of Dr. Richard Louis Miller / Angela Brown-Miller.
       p.   cm. — (Frontiers in psychotherapy)
   Includes bibliographical references.
   ISBN 0-89391-904-7 (cl.) — ISBN 0-89391-905-5 (pbk.)
   1. Substance abuse—Treatment. 2. Group Psychotherapy.
3. Gestalt therapy. 4. Miller, Richard Louis. I. Title.
II. Series: Frontiers in psychotherapy series.
   [DNLM: 1. Gestalt Therapy. 2. Psychotherapy, Group—methods.
3. Substance Abuse—Therapy. 4. Substance Dependence—Therapy.   WM
270 B883g 1993]
RC564.B78 1993
616.86'0651—dc20
DNLM/DLC
for Library of Congress   93-12291
                                                                                        CIP

Ablex Publishing Corporation
355 Chestnut Street
Norwood, New Jersey 07648

To Richard

Contents

Acknowledgments

I wish to thank the many people who have made this project possible. Among them are Susan Barrera, who for many years has been a faithful friend and expert word processor, even under the greatest of duress, and Heidi Beeler, who pulled this manuscript together, combining her editorial and word-processing talents in the face of inevitable deadlines.

Also among them are the staff members of the Cokenders Alcohol and Drug Program and the Wilbur Hot Springs Health Sanctuary in Williams, California, whose dedicated work has made and continues to make a profound mark in the history of human caring and curing. And I must, of course, thank the patients who were participants in the group therapy sessions and who submitted poetry and autobiographies for this project. They will not be individually named in this acknowledgment out of respect for confidentiality. (Their names have been changed in the text for the same reason.) These people have spilled their guts and bared their souls and then shared this process. I thank them from the bottom of my heart for their sharing and their vigilance.

And I thank, along with his patients, my friend, partner, and colleague, Dr. Richard Louis Miller, without whom the events described in this book would not have occurred. His contribution to so many people's healings, and his contribution to the fields of addiction, psychotherapy, and health care, have made an unforgettable difference in all our lives.

About the Author

Angela Browne-Miller holds two masters degrees (one in public health and one in social welfare) and two doctorates (one in social welfare and one in education) from the University of California at Berkeley, where she serves as a lecturer. Dr. Browne-Miller is a licensed clinical social worker in California, where she has worked with chemically dependent children, adolescents, and adults in residential, outpatient, and corporate settings. She has done extensive consulting with corporations experiencing drug and alcohol problems. She has developed and presented special seminars on employee substance abuse and addiction and other workplace mental health issues for businesses, community organizations, and the University of California at Berkeley, where she teaches the first course on employee assistance ever offered at that campus.

Dr. Browne-Miller's areas of research and publication include psychotherapy, social policy, employee assistance, addiction, working women, and day-care. Her writing has been published nationally and internationally in the lay and the professional press. She has discussed her work on national and local television and radio, and at conferences and institutes, including the National Broadcasters' Association, the Aspen Institute, Esalen, Californians for Drug Free Youth, the California State Psychological Association, and the American Academy of Psychotherapists. She has served as a member of the U.S. Office of Juvenile Justice Task Force on Drug Abuse, as a Lecturer at the University of California at Berkeley, and as a National Institute of Mental Health Postdoctoral Fellow. Dr. Browne-Miller co-authored with her husband the newspaper column, *MILLER & MILLER*, and co-hosted the accompanying radio show, which was carried on fifteen stations, MILLER AND MILLER ON HEALTH AND PSYCHOLOGY. Other books by Dr. Browne-Miller include *The Day Care Dilemma* (Plenum, 1990), *Working Dazed* (Plenum, 1991), *Raising Our Children's Intelligence* (Plenum, 1994), and *Transcending Addiction and Other Afflictions* (Ablex, 1993).

1

Introduction to Gestalting Addiction

drugs for everyday living
drugs for everyday pain
drugs for every situation
God, this is insane

living for everyday drugs
paining for everyday life
damn all these drugs here before me
and let me get back to my wife

a story of life full of darkness
deeper and uglier than sin
one that i've shared with my brothers
and now i can say i can win

i can win

(Anonymous Group Therapy Participant)

When I first met Richard Louis Miller in the early 1970s, he was a psychologist with a dream of building a healing community. He had closed a very successful clinic in San Francisco and purchased a natural hot springs, with accompanying Victorian hotel and 240-acre private valley, in Northern California. I met Richard at the hotel. He was working. He already had patients coming to see him in this secluded healing environment. Many of these patients lived on the grounds and participated in long-term residential treatment for various serious psychological conditions. Some of them were people whose families had been told that they would have to be institutionalized for the rest of their lives. Dr. Miller provided a nonhospital treatment that enabled them to return to society and enjoy productive lives.

I knew quite a bit about what has been called *milieu therapy*, but I had never seen a milieu quite like this place, Wilbur Hot Springs. And although still in its developmental stages, the overlay of a unique working and healing community, headed by a psychologist, was already quite special.

As did many other health professionals, I began to use Richard Miller's hot springs as an occasional personal retreat, a place where I could go to rejuvenate and to direct my own healing energy. I made frequent weekend visits and grew to depend on this injection of life energy for sustenance. When I encountered serious physical health problems of my own in the mid-1970s, visits to this healing environment were like pilgrimages to a metaphorical source. There were occasions when, being unable to get to Wilbur for long periods of time, I found that just imagining myself there was helpful.

I spent a couple of years facing the challenge of a debilitating neurological disease. When I finally pulled my body and my life back together, I recognized the depth of the spiritual, creative, emotional, and intellectual energy that I had tapped into for my healing. I understood the profound gift, the high-level lesson, that my healing had offered me. I felt it was essential that I turn around and share my healing energy with others who needed it.

But what would be the avenue for returning the gift? I had worked with "disturbed" and "addicted" children and adolescents in residential treatment communities prior to falling ill. Now that I had fallen well, I thought of returning to work in residential treatment, but I wanted to find an opportunity to work with adults, my peers. I spent some years looking for the appropriate avenue. I was not surprised when Wilbur Hot Springs, an environment that had, so often, offered me healing, now offered me an opportunity to help others heal. I saw that Richard had started an addiction treatment program at Wilbur. I approached him with the idea that I work with him and write a book about the work.

That same day, he invited me to sit in on the group therapy he was doing with his addicted patients. I accepted the invitation. It took but a few moments for me to see the special magic, the healing alchemy, that

Richard was able to bring out in this circle of people who had come for help. I was immediately struck by the power, the force of his work. I saw that he was gestalting addiction. He was calling addiction out of each patient, asking it to make itself visible and to allow the group members to see it, hear it, feel it—to better know it—to complete their pictures of it. He was gently urging the fragments of each of his patients' addictions out of obscurity and into the contexts of the whole persons and the whole society in which they had actually originated.

Indeed, as addiction came out into the room, the picture of the monster—the addiction—became more whole. The circle closed itself like a completed circuit. I could feel the energy, the synergy, of heightened group awareness. The result of this intense gestalting process was at once profound and subtle. Some of the profound effects were immediately obvious. Others were slow to emerge and yet very powerful. People-changing was happening. And most of the people who began to change in profound ways in those groups continue, years afterward, to change in profound ways today. All of us, helpers and helpees alike, were able to walk away from those groups feeling that we had encountered something very real and starkly naked about the human condition.

Some years after we began working together, Richard and I married. Not long after that, we had a child. She was invited to enough group therapy sessions to acquire an understanding of methods of directing groups and bringing out feelings. She often tries to lead us, when seated around the dinner table, in a group therapy session. A few years ago, one of our babysitters asked us what caused her to "hit the chair like that." It took us a moment to realize that she had incorporated into her own life the practical methods of venting anger and other feelings that she had learned in watching group therapy. She was performing a simple therapeutic exercise.

Graduates of the groups you will read about in this book have also incorporated into their lives the methodologies of gestalt. They have learned to express feelings that were once locked into their life patterns, the patterns that invited addiction. They have learned to close the circle of what was once broken communication with the self and with others.

I have written this book to share an experience, my experience, of Richard Miller's great work. It is my hope that psychotherapists and other health professionals, as well as patients, clients, and anyone else who reads the following chapters, will gain an understanding of the complexity and power of addiction-focused group therapy. It is my intention to have *Gestalting Addiction* serve as documentation of a valuable and effective approach to people-changing.

This approach was forged by Dr. Miller out of his knowledge of, and experience with, gestalt therapy and his deep understanding of psychological problems including schizophrenia, obsessive compulsive disorders, phobias, eating disorders, and addictions. You will see the influences of the founder of Gestalt Therapy, psychiatrist Fritz Perls, of whom Richard was a student and a colleague, and of the founder of Family Systems Therapy, social worker Virginia Satir, with whom Richard led groups at Esalen.

You will have to read *between* the lines herein to learn about the wonderfully astute and sensitive way Richard leads his therapy groups. He directs and works with collections of shifting feelings and energies in the circle as if he were the conductor and his patients members of the orchestra. The rich passages, overtures, and themes are brought to full crescendo, heard well, and played to completion. The harmonies and disharmonies are coaxed and pulled from the souls of circle members. One begins to feel that there is nothing that happens in the world, no passion, no absence of passion, no feeling of any sort, that is not played out in the circle. Among them, these addicted people have experienced the gamut of human pathos—and it can be gestalted.

PART I

CALLING ADDICTION OUT OF HIDING

2

Teaching Wellness and Wholeness: The Cokenders Alcohol and Drug Program Story

It is a long way home.
Will anyone ever live there again?

(Anonymous Group Therapy Participant)

The *drug problem* is not going away. Sometimes a popular drug loses in the public relations competition and another takes its place, but the *drug problem* just keeps resurfacing.

During the 1980s it was cocaine. Cocaine found its way into almost every nook and cranny of American life. The smallest town and the largest city had cocaine available for sale. The users were bankers and barbers, contractors and chemists, truck drivers and chief executive officers, nuclear power plant operators and farmers, race drivers and doctors, homemakers and computer experts. They came from all walks of life, all socioeconomic groups, and they had one behavior in common:

They used cocaine. Having this single behavior in common facilitated their being able to look beyond their many differences in order to form a subculture of snorters, smokers, injectors, and drinkers of one of the world's most insidious drugs. The number of cocaine users, and the number of cocaine addicts, soared during the 1980s. And now, in the nineties, as new "lab" drugs are invented, making available new highs at lowered prices, some of these drugs may follow a course similar to cocaine's.

One day in the winter of 1982, in California, a physician called Dr. Richard Louis Miller and said that his house guest was "freaking out." Several hours later the "freaked out" house guest and her husband were in Dr. Miller's office, telling their story. The wife had been experiencing hallucinations. She had seen fire-breathing monsters standing in the doorway of her home, and her husband's decapitated head on a ski pole in the closet. She was plagued by the thought that people were trying to break into her house. She had been to a local psychiatrist, who had put her on Valium. This psychiatrist never bothered to interview her about her drug use and abuse. Had he done so, he would have found out that she was taking quaaludes and cocaine on a regular basis. What she was experiencing was *cocaine psychosis*, a well-known phenomenon among cocaine users. Dr. Miller took her off all mind-altering substances, treated her with a combination of psychotherapy and milieu therapy, and encouraged a lot of family support. Her hallucinations quickly passed. She was able to change her drug habits and resume a healthy life.

Several weeks later, Dr. Miller received a call from a friend telling him that his young bride had just died. Dr. Miller was shocked. "How did she die?" "I think it was too much cocaine," said his friend. The autopsy confirmed his suspicion. The young woman had suffered a cardiac arrest brought on by sniffing less than a gram of cocaine. Soon after that, Dr. Miller began to design what was to become the first treatment program that was exclusively for cocaine users—*cokers*. Within two years, it was apparent that the majority of the cocaine users who enrolled in Dr. Miller's in- and outpatient programs were also using alcohol or other drugs. And as word got around that this program, *Cokenders*, treated addiction, many people with marijuana, alcohol, and other primary addictions asked if they might enroll and were accepted into the program.

This program thus became the *Cokenders Alcohol and Drug Program*. From the start, its theoretical orientation was humanistic and holistic. Rather than set the first residential or inpatient component of his program in a hospital, Dr. Miller began Cokenders in a very special type of healing environment: his own Wilbur Hot Springs Health Sanctuary, located in an idyllic private valley about 110 miles northeast of San Francisco. In the years since its inception, the value of the nonhospital milieu in addiction treatment has gone from being a controversial issue to being an almost irrefutable one.

THE ROLE OF ENVIRONMENT
IN TREATING ADDICTION

Wilbur Hot Springs has a long history. The springs were once a sacred healing ground for Native Americans. Later, in the late 19th and early 20th centuries, Wilbur became an international curing spa. Wilbur Hot Springs is now a sanctuary used by members of the public to rest, away from the tempo of modern life. It is a place where people of all walks of life go to *destress before* the get a *dis*-ease. The physical environment is pristine. The secluded Wilbur Hot Springs valley is five miles from the nearest blacktop highway and twenty-two miles from the nearest town. The air is untouched by industrialization, and the noise level is below that of a library. The staff share a philosophy that is in accord with the credo of humanistic philosophy: "an affirmation of the fundamental uniqueness and importance of each and all human life" and a recognition that "no matter how he or she is labeled or evaluated, a person is a human being first of all and most deeply."

Many of Wilbur's early 20th-century visitors left behind their canes, crutches, and wheel chairs, feeling that they were leaving their physical disabilities behind after spending time in that special healing environment. In the 1980s, Richard Miller brought people with another type of disabling problem, chemical dependence, to Wilbur to heal. They, too, left behind their crutches—their drugs and their paraphernalia.

Within the physical and emotional safety and security of Wilbur, a profound healing process was initiated. By clearing away the external physical and psychological distractions of the modern world, Dr. Miller was able to direct the energies of his clients toward rebalancing—restoring their emotional, physical, and spiritual balances. He was able to construct what one participant called a "brief eternity"—an intense life-changing experience. The road to health and away from addiction must begin in a safe, calm, secure, and human setting. This is why Dr. Miller chose Wilbur as the first setting for his treatment program.

THE ROLE OF LOVE, DIGNITY, AND
HUMANITY IN TREATMENT

Cokenders began as an idea about how to help people with cocaine addiction when most of society had not yet heard that cocaine was addictive. The program emerged as a highly original model for "treating" all of society by working with some of its members, its "identified patients," those who were manifesting symptoms of what is actually a societal-level disturbance. Cokenders was designed to help make people whole and human again after they had been hurt—hurt badly—in a world that tends to fragment and dehumanize people. The power of love, dignity, and humanity that has worked on program participants cannot be captured in words—it must be experienced by the heart.

Since its inception in August 1982, the program has worked with some 1,500 patients addicted to cocaine, alcohol, prescription medicine, and other drugs, along with many of their family members and significant others, as well as with people suffering from eating and other behavioral addictions. Not one of those people has been hospitalized or medicated since. Dr. Miller's nonhospital, medicine-free, psychotherapeutic approach to addiction treatment has proved highly effective. In 1990, the Cokenders Alcohol and Drug Program joined the Parkside Medical Services network. Parkside is one of the country's oldest and largest nonprofit addiction treatment programs in the U.S. The exciting process of bringing an alternative form of addiction treatment into the mainstream began. Dr. Richard Miller has offered the national health care system humanistic addiction treatment.

I have put this book together to celebrate the emergence of Dr. Richard Miller's treatment model and to emphasize the central role played by group psychotherapy, particularly gestalt therapy, in this model. I want to share with readers the intensity, clarity, sensitivity, and beauty of expression that I have witnessed in the group therapy sessions led by Dr. Miller. The contents of this book are both a tribute to the participants and to Richard Miller.[1]

---

[1] Outcome data that demonstrate the effectiveness of Dr. Miller's holistic treatment design (including psychotherapy, exercise, nutrition, relaxation, and education) are available in Angela Browne-Miller, *Working Dazed* (Plenum, 1991) and Angela Browne, "New Perspectives in Chemical Dependence Treatment Evaluation," *Employee Assistance Quarterly*, Vol. 4, No. 2 (March 1989).

*"I don't care what I have to do
if it gets me off coke, I'll do it."*

3

The Value of Dialogue

I can hear myself feeling,
but I sound
so far away.

(Anonymous Group Therapy Participant)

Personal and social change for the better depends upon honest communication. Dishonest communication is worse than no communication at all. There is much to be learned about the way we do and do not communicate from the words of addicted individuals. Addicted individuals may actually be leading the way into this learning for everyone. Their immediate survival depends upon this learning. So does everyone else's survival; our need only *appears* to be less immediate.

It is so easy to say, "This isn't you, this is the drugs[1] talking" to an addict. Yet drugs are inanimate collections of chemicals with no minds of their own. Drugs do not talk; people do. When people who are under the influence of a drug (either "on drugs" or "craving drugs" or "withdrawing from drugs" or "hung over") say something out of character or "act like an addict" or a "drug fiend," *they* are doing the talking, not their drugs. Yet

---

[1] Alcohol is a drug and is included in the use of this term herein.

the words are not saying everything that might be said about their needs or their conditions or their feelings. This is because drugs enable their users to mask, camouflage, or even distort emotions, ideas, and judgments.

When the addicted person is talking, what is he or she really saying, and what is it that is not being said? When the complications, pressures, confusions, rewards, pleasures, and insights that are part of daily life feel overwhelming, drugs provide a *chemical denial barrier*—or *false escape*. When daily life is not stimulating enough, drugs provide a sense of stimulation. When daily life is overstimulating, drugs provide a *chemical hideout*. When something hurts too much, drugs *numb the pain*. When something does not hurt enough, drugs *exaggerate the pain*. Addicts are telling us so much more than "I want to use drugs." They are saying that:

1. Their coping mechanisms feel untrained and inadequate—hence drugs are their crutches; and that,
2. They cannot communicate all that they are feeling to others or even to themselves; and,
3. Above all, they are saying, *"Help"*.

How do we learn to hear the addict cry "help"? How do addicts learn to hear themselves? And how do we learn to hear ourselves cry "help"? Communication skills are essential tools in the treatment of addiction: the addicted person and the therapist must unearth and listen to otherwise buried, numbed, distorted, disorganized, and unfelt or unconsciously felt feeling. Addicted people, living inside a maze of their own making, a chemical prison, can map their own routes to freedom, can form the key that releases them from their own jails. The therapist can only facilitate this process. Yes, the addicted individual *can* be guided, but he or she *must make his or her own way*. Similarly, every person, whether addicted or not, *can* be guided toward truth, but he or she, too, *must make his or her own way*. Remember that truth is the only *real* communication.

WORKING WITH PEOPLE WHO ARE ADDICTED

The concepts of content and process are central in gestalt therapy. In Chapters 3, 4, and 5 you will see that Dr. Miller persistently attends to the differentiation of content and process, of the lyrics and the music.

When things do not go well, people become critical of the content of themselves or of their environments and believe that they have to change this content for things to go better. Attempts to change or alter "content" may be constructive or destructive. An addicted person's use of drugs in an effort to change content is *de*structive. Destructive dependence upon a mind- and mood-altering drug grows when the drug user's efforts to change what he or she perceives as "content" are not actually effective, but are repeated anyway. Time after time, drugs are used, and time after time, they do not solve problems: When the users comes back to reality, its content is the same. The problems that they used drugs to escape from are still there. Yet, they return to the drugs in search of the fleeting illusion of escape from the content of reality.

Chemically dependent people, just as almost everyone else, pay a great deal of attention to content. This is a factor that must be overcome in group therapy. Many addicted individuals arrive at group therapy unaware (i.e., trying to make other people responsible for their problems, slipping out of confrontation with their own emotional patterns, and playing these games without admitting or even knowing it). Manipulations and games are very much a part of addiction: Addiction says content must be operated upon, manipulated, at any cost.

No matter how much of the process the therapist can see, addicted individuals have to decide for themselves when to really "work," when to fully participate in group therapy. Some participants play "discover me" in groups; they cry quietly, or sigh in a corner, or send out a message, covert or overt, to get attention. The therapist can comment on this habit; he or she can point out that this behavior is occurring and has probably occurred elsewhere in life. However, the goal of group therapy with addicted persons is to generate self-awareness. As Dr. Miller explains, simply *interpreting* a patient's behavior *to* the patient is not enough. *Helping* patients with their real problems is a subtle task. Patients must be led into self-recognition.

The group therapy sessions conducted during the residential week of the Cokenders Alcohol and Drug Program reveal the nature of Dr. Miller's therapeutic facilitation and its interlinking with therapeutic teaching. I have included actual and fabricated transcripts of selected sessions conducted by Dr. Miller. These *scripts*, or dialogues, reveal a great deal about how addicted individuals communicate and feel about themselves. These dialogues are also quite instructive regarding the work of the therapist. The next three chapters have been edited and organized around the concepts and exercises presented in these group therapy sessions and listed below. These are:

In Chapter 4, "Learning to Go Conscious,"

• The *Breathing Exercise* teaches the power of controlled breathing in reducing tension and anxiety, promoting self-control, and generating a relaxed state.

- *The Sensory Awareness Exercise* demonstrates the power of developing a keener awareness of what the body is feeling as it experiences emotion.
- *The Unfinished Business Exercise* allows its user to release feelings (music) and comments (lyrics) directed at other people that he or she may have buried deep inside himself.
- *The Semantic Awareness Exercise* encourages a closer awareness of word choice (lyrics) and of what is being said in order to better hear the feelings (music) and messages behind the words.

In Chapter 5, "Undrugging the Feelings,"

- *Breaking Through Deceits* is an important experience for a person who wants to break addiction, because heightened awareness of one's denial and deceit is an important step in learning real self-control.
- *Identifying and Connecting Cravings* must be done to the fullest in order for an addicted person to realize that he or she can crave various drugs without using any of them.
- *Giving Full Voice to Buried Feelings* is essential in the healing of pent-up hurts and old wounds and in preventing the dangerous storage of new but unexpressed hurts and wounds.
- *Meeting the Addict* is something the addicted person knows how to do but rarely has the opportunity to do in a therapeutic setting.
- *Seeing Family and Personal Relationships* is also a process that is simple but beneficial for the addicted person.

In Chapter 6, "Leaving Chemical Dependence Behind: The Longest Goodbye,"

- *Desensitization* is a process that teaches addicted persons to "reprogram" their habitual responses to the objects of their addictions.
- *Making a New Beginning* is a concept that allows participants to believe that it is, indeed, possible to start again and that it *is* reasonable to *hope. Hope and the sharing of hope heals.*

These exercises and concepts are presented to addicted persons in the group therapy context to allow them to use and master these "tools" while working in a group and dealing with the multiple dynamics of a group therapy setting. Patients are often overtly or covertly resistant to learning and/or applying specific skills and knowledge to their addiction problems. This is why a good portion of all education and training offered in addiction treatment must be offered in a therapeutic environment such as that provided by Dr. Miller. However, more than a set of exercises and concepts is presented in the following three chapters. The group therapy environment provides a grounding, in a safe setting peopled by peers, for the risk taking of intense therapeutic expression. In working with addicted persons, a keenly facilitated group therapy process offers a magic all of its own. Individuals change. The group changes. And then the world is a new and healthier place for them and for everyone to be in. Join us now as we dialogue with addiction.

"*Drugs are chemical crutches.*"

4

Learning to Go Conscious

I faced my future as I stood and stared
Yet, out of the darkness there came
Another image of myself to see
With features exactly the same
All at once it became so clear
My life was really on the line
I knew that if I really wanted to live
I'd have to see my life as mine

(Anonymous Group Therapy Participant)

This is the first of three chapters drawn from transcripts of Dr. Miller's group therapy sessions. I have edited, condensed, and pieced together these actual and fabricated transcripts in order to highlight specific elements of Dr. Miller's method. All of these transcripts were made with the participating patients' permissions. I have changed names wherever necessary.

Patients are taught in the group to focus on their physical, social, and psychological processes. Their emotional responses to this focusing are worked on in the group. In clearing the blocks to their focusing, patients can gain control—*go conscious*—in their combat with addiction, and they can share the process with others.

What the members of Dr. Miller's addiction therapy groups have in common with many other people is their inattention to the warning signals—the cries of pain—coming from their psyches and bodies. I find Dr. Miller's work essential in an era in which we are becoming more mechanical and less human. One of the most significant features of his therapeutic style is his attention to the expression of deeply buried feelings—unheeded physical sensations and emotions. It is critical that all people learn to heed their emotions, to recognize that these are their own warning signals—to know their feelings when they are having them. Otherwise, we all risk losing touch with our feelings and therefore our humanity. Otherwise, we risk falling prey to extreme forms of social domination and control that are more appropriate for use with unfeeling machines. Addiction is one of these forms of control.

The following group therapy participants are being taught exercises to help them become more conscious of—recognize—their innermost physical and emotional signals. Although most of them are struggling with addictions, their issues are representative of many other people's special issues. These dialogues occurred during group therapy sessions conducted by Dr. Richard Miller. Follow along as these people learn to *go conscious*. We will begin with a very elementary but essential exercise. Note how Dr. Miller allows the dialogue to flow to related subjects.

BREATHING EXERCISE

Controlled breathing, which Dr. Miller adapted from various meditation methods, is valuable in reducing tension and generating relaxation. With practice, the effectiveness of controlled breathing is enhanced. And as one gains control over an automatic process such as breathing, a greater sense of self-awareness, self-consciousness and self-control is developed. This is an especially valuable development in impulse and addiction control. Addicted persons who wish to gain greater control over their behaviors can use breathing in coping with high-pressure situations and in getting through the stressful moments (or hours or days) of craving the drugs or objects of their addictions. Below, Dr. Miller teaches breathing to group members. Note that this breathing is not easy to learn, as indicated by Susan's comments (i.e., "I don't even feel myself breathing"). The therapist teaching this breathing method does well to offer many opportunities to practice and to apply the technique in the context of group psychotherapy. A group setting allows participants to watch each other learn.

Dr. Miller: When I am asked to name the psychological tool that does the most for me, I name the one that I think is the most powerful—

LEARNING TO GO CONSCIOUS • 21

breathing. And so I'm going to start off this morning by teaching you a breathing exercise that you can use here, and at home, quite beneficially.

To begin with, believe it or not, many of us breathe improperly. This might sound a little bit surprising to you, since we all breathe, and you wonder how could we possibly learn to breathe improperly, since it's an automatic function. Yet, somewhere along the line, many of us have learned to hold our stomachs tight, and to breathe up here, in the chest. The classic of this is the Marine's style of breathing: stomach in, chest out: you hold the entire stomach area tight. Of course, when I hold this whole area tight, I get uptight, which sends messages through my entire system that I'm tight.

What I want to do is offer you a tool to use when you get uptight, to loosen yourself and to send a message to your entire system that everything is stabilized, that everything is getting back to homeostasis, that you're not in a panic situation, and that you don't have to reach for your favorite drug or drugs in order to stabilize everything.

I'll demonstrate by placing my hand over my stomach, so you can see my stomach move—(it's really my abdomen, the lower section of my torso). I want you to practice this: hold your chest area constant, very little movement, and move the abdomen to breathe. Abdominal breathing is the goal.

One way to practice this, in the beginning, is to move your stomach in and out without using breath, just using the muscles, to get familiar with that area. You can do this slowly, and then, after you've gotten the feel of it, concentrate on using this method to breathe. Pull the breath down into the lower lobes of the lungs.

[The group practices this exercise.]

This exercise will beat Valium for relaxation and for rapidity of action, because you can relax more deeply and more rapidly with this than you can with a pill.

How are you doing there, Tom? Feel the movement? Susan, you got it?

Susan: I can't even feel anything.

Dr. Miller: You can't feel anything yet? Sort of generally numb all over? This numbness is very typical of a freebaser's withdrawal from cocaine.

Susan: I don't even feel myself breathing right now.

Dr. Miller: Give it time, you've got the muscle movement, that's a good start.

Susan: Now how do I breathe while doing this muscle stuff?

Dr. Miller: Make that abdominal muscle move in and out. Now, bring your breath down to move your abdomen. Keep your chest still. Breathe through the back of your nostrils. Sit back in your chair. Put your hand on your abdomen and make it move with the breath. You're starting to get it right. Much smoother, now, give it a little fluidity instead of jerking like that. Less chest. Hardly move up here [Dr. Miller pats his chest]. There, you just started to get it there. Did you feel it when you got it? Okay, a little less chest movement now.

Susan: I did feel it that one time.

Dr. Miller: You're going to have to practice this. I've been practicing for fifteen years. It helps to lie down to practice, too. It is easier than standing up.

The next thing I want all of you to do, while you're doing this breathing exercise, is to take your fingertips and very gently explore the entire soft area from the bottom of your ribs right down to your pelvis with your fingers. You start out by going gently, and then deeper and deeper. Do this one with your eyes closed the first couple of times. The reason for that is I want you to focus on the inside, not to get distracted by looking at somebody. What you're doing now is you're looking in with your fingertips, with your mind's eye, and just checking for any tight spots that are in there, all the while. Looking at the area with your mind's eye, your inner periscope, will allow you to find any sensitive or tight spots, any tight muscles or any compactions, and to alleviate them. Anybody getting a tight muscle or a tight spot in there? You are, Jim?

Jim: Say some more about what you mean by "sensitive."

Dr. Miller: Well, that's a message that something wants some kind of attention. If you are getting a message of high sensitivity in a particular spot, something is going on there. One of the many difficulties with drugging heavily, and, especially in your case, with using your drug, cocaine, is that the messages that you are continuously receiving from your body get cut off. You get one general message when you're on coke: stimulation. Remember, cocaine has two specific physical effects. First, it's a central nervous system stimulant—it stimulates the entire system; it's like taking one of the wires entering the house carrying electricity and putting more electricity into it. We've got our own electrical system that's going on all the time, our own neurochemical system. When we throw in a little coke, it goes right to the brain, interacts with the neurotransmitters—the information transmitters in the brain—and hypes up the entire system. Second, coke is a topical anesthetic: put it on a particular spot and it anesthetizes that spot. When you take it in other ways, such as "freebasing," you're generalizing the effect of the anesthesia. You've been cutting yourselves off from your own information systems. Many times you'll take the coke and won't even feel particular areas of your body. In fact, many times one takes coke and doesn't feel *any* areas of one's body—instead one feels a general vibration. It'll be interesting to see, as you pay more attention to your insides, what happens with this sensitive

What cocaine does

abdominal area. I encourage all of you to practice the breathing exercise at various times during the day. Now, Susan, how long has it been since you last used a drug?

Susan: Almost 72 hours. The last drug was coke.

Dr. Miller: Now, Susan's system is saying, "Enough, don't jack me up again with that chemical, I need a chance to just relax here and to rebuild." But while Susan is going through this rebuilding, she may feel depression and unhappiness.

Tom: How long does it take for the body to rebuild, or to replenish the natural energy that it has totally used up?

Dr. Miller: Well, that's a good question. The body, I mean, the human organism, is fantastic. And you know, when it comes to coke it's just miraculous. The coke—most of it is out of your system within 24 hours. Within 72 hours, well over 90%, conservatively, is out of your system. And so as soon as you stop pumping it in, your body is already starting to rebuild. I can't be positive of this, but there is a strong likelihood that you, Susan, will be feeling very differently by tomorrow morning, and extremely different by the next day. Jim, you have something to say about this.

Jim: Yeah. I was extremely tired the first three days of the program, and it seemed like there were two different plateaus that—actually, now I'm going through another plateau. There's a short term buildup, it feels like, and within three days there was a big difference. I wasn't fighting sleep constantly. And even now I notice—it may be just because I'm more relaxed—but there are times I can lie down and take a nap. I've never been able to do that in my life. But I still feel like I'm not back to having that original reserve.

Tom: I know I was tired after five minutes of stretching class today. I mean seriously tired, and felt my muscles tired, aching, sore. [Tom refers to the stretching class Dr. Miller offers during his week-long intensive program.]

Dr. Miller: Good! You're starting to *feel* your muscles.

Tom: Yeah, it's a little painful, and yet it's good pain. It's real.

Dr. Miller: Real…to be feeling tired after five minutes.

Tom: Honestly. They were simple movements that she was showing us, and I asked (and I wasn't trying to be funny), "Should this be a tiring movement?" We were not even moving at that point, we were just in a particular stretching position.

Dr. Miller: Yes. Well, there is hardly an exercise, that should make a man of your musculature tired after doing it for a few minutes.

Tom: I should be in a little better condition than that, right? Yeah.

Dr. Miller: Something's going on with you, and it's not your muscles.

Tom: Correct, right.

Dr. Miller: Right. Tension is tiring you. What many of us do is we tense up and stay that way. We forget to relax. We're in a board room, and somebody attacks us, or at work, and some other colleague says something, or we're in a physical situation and somebody makes a threatening motion—some kind of threatening situation: Many of us have a habit of tensing, setting ourselves for the onslaught. We tense our muscles, tense our stomachs. You all can get another kind of habit established, which is a habit of being able to loosen yourselves up in the tense situations that you want to loosen yourselves up in, rather than being compulsively in that pattern of tightening. Remember, tension takes energy. You want to breathe easier and oxygenate your blood. Oxygen is one of our main energy sources. And that's what this whole exercise is about: keeping your muscles loose and sending a message of looseness to the system, and oxygenating rather than holding your breath. Remember, the heart is a pump, and the pump works by electricity; the heart pumps blood to the lungs, and the lungs put oxygen, which is an essential fuel, into the body's energy system, into the blood. The blood comes back up to the heart, and once again it's pumped out to the body, and in the blood is our oxygen—energy.

So there's a lot involved in this one little exercise. It's simple to do, it takes practice, and it has far-reaching effects. It's worth spending quite a bit of time on.

Tom: Immediate effects! This exercise has changed my whole mood.

Clara: Is this exercise frustrating to anyone else but me?

[The group is silent.]

Dr. Miller: Well, I do the exercise often. It's taken me time to have a natural belly, a relaxed belly. I had to work to get myself to relax. Just be patient with yourself. It'll come.

Clara: I find that difficult.

Dr. Miller: Being patient with yourself?

Tom: Developing good habits.

Clara: That too.

GESTALT SENSORY AWARENESS EXERCISE

The sensory awareness exercise is a prelude to other gestalt exercises. Increased awareness is essential in overriding automatic behaviors. The more aware one is of critical bodily cues—hints that an automatic response to particular triggers is about to begin or is already in progress—the more power one has to override automatic responses.

In this section, Dr. Miller demonstrates to the group an exercise in sensory awareness. When preparing a group for intense emotional work, this is a good opening exercise. This exercise allows its users to link emotions with physical sensations, and vice versa, as a means of heightening perceptions of both. Given that it is the nature of many chemically dependent people to turn off their physical and emotional sensations (especially physical and emotional pain), it is a good idea to repeat an exercise such as this one at several points during group therapy. During his week-long residential program (which includes five hours of group therapy per day), Dr. Miller begins almost every group with this exercise. I have included a discussion that evolved out of the introduction of these exercises. Note that the participants in addiction-focused group psychotherapy play a major role in maintaining the group's focus on addiction. They often turn generic exercises and dialogues into addiction-focused ones. This is made even more effective by a therapist who can explicitly tie such a discussion into the exercise being studied, as does Dr. Miller at the end of this section.

Dr. Miller: Now, the awareness exercise. Susan, I'll start with you, use you as the demonstration. And it's very easy. All I want you to do is finish this sentence. "I am most aware of..." and then finish the sentence with something about your body.

Susan: I am most aware of my stomach right now.

Dr. Miller: Okay. All right, that's the beginning of this exercise. It's the beginning of paying attention to bodily cues. Now we'll get more specific. What about your stomach? What is the message that your stomach is sending?

Susan: It hurts. Right here on the side, right here it hurts.

Dr. Miller: Okay. Now we're going from "I am aware of my stomach" to "I am aware of pain in my stomach." More specific—from the general to the specific. Then Susan also went a little further and went to the particular area, which is the next step, from the general "my stomach" to "pain in my stomach" to where the pain is located. Where is the pain located in your stomach?

Susan: Well, it's really the side, right here. Left.

Dr. Miller: Okay. Can you describe what kind of pain it is? Is it a pressing pain, or a sharp pain?

Susan: I'm thinking about it.

Dr. Miller: Again, I'm going to ask you to finish the sentence, "I am most aware of..." and do it with your eyes closed, and tell me what you're most aware of internally.

Susan: I can feel pressure on my chest like the [breathing deeply], like I smoked too much coke or too many cigarettes, or something.

Dr. Miller: Okay. Thank You. That's the exercise. As simple as that.

Susan: I'm done?

Dr. Miller: Yeah. [Laughter.] You can relax now. Lou? Say the sentence, "I am most aware of…"

Lou: I am most aware of my neck, my shoulders, and my back.

Dr. Miller: Okay. Let's start with your neck. What about your neck are you most aware of?

Lou: When I turn my head, I feel like vertebrae are rubbing against each other. I even hear a little—not a crack, more like a "clunk."

Dr. Miller: And your shoulders? What are you most aware of about your shoulders?

Lou: Stiffness running through.

Dr. Miller: Okay. Let's do the same exercise now with your eyes closed. Close your eyes. Catch the first thing that pops into you mind.

Lou: I'm most aware of my breathing.

Dr. Miller: Okay. Now get more specific. What are you aware of?

Lou: Well, I've been practicing for two weeks with deep stomach breathing, so I'm still very conscious of—breathing isn't natural—I'm still very conscious of making sure it's in my stomach.

Dr. Miller: Thank you. Tom?

Tom: I'm most aware of a pain in my chest also….I mean, there is a pain that I can feel in the back, and there is a pain connected to it that I can feel in the chest.

Dr. Miller: You mean it goes right through you, the pain?

Tom: Yeah. It goes right into the center, and right out the center of my back.

Dr. Miller: Okay. Let's do the same exercise now with your eyes closed. What do you see when you breathe now?

Tom: It's…my breathing, and it's a feeling of oxygen, oxygenating, …It's cool and clean and beautiful and life-giving.

Dr. Miller: Susan?

Susan: I haven't been conscious long enough to tell what I'm aware of. If I close my eyes, I'll go to sleep.

Dr. Miller: That's okay.

Susan: I've gone to sleep in everything I've done today, so I don't…I'm just more aware of my exhaustion.

Dr. Miller: Uh-huh. That's real important.

Susan: Yeah. And staying awake is too.

Dr. Miller: That's real important. And by the way, once you're here, in this meeting, if you want to close your eyes, and that's what your body wants is to let itself go to sleep, go right ahead.

Susan: I've done it three times already! It just happened!

Dr. Miller: Well, it's perfectly okay with me. You will not sleep the entire week. You may sleep more in the beginning.

Susan: For no reason these naps start, for no reason they stop. I've been through with cocaine for weeks. I haven't ever been this tired, through. Normally by now I would've gone out and bought some more. I don't allow myself to become this tired.

Dr. Miller: Phil? "I am most aware of…"?

Phil: As far as the addiction to cocaine, I am most aware of the total abuse that I have put my body through.

Dr. Miller: What are you most aware of in your body right at this very second? What do you notice about yourself?

Phil: Uh…Actually, at this moment, I feel better about myself and my body than I have for some time.

Dr. Miller: Say more about this, Phil.

Phil: The eyes aren't quite as bad as they used to be, and they, they were absolutely terrible. I couldn't stand to look at myself in the mirror. The nose isn't quite as sensitive, I can almost touch it now, and it's bearable—before, it wasn't bearable at all. I can almost blow my nose again and not expect it to be bleeding. You know, I've got a long, long, long way to go, but…certainly I've taken a step forward.

Dr. Miller: What do you see now? Close your eyes now, and tell me what you see on the television screen inside your mind.

Phil: On the television screen?

Dr. Miller: Whatever you call the picture tube—it's either black and white or it's color, or there's nothing on it, or there's a picture or a sensation on it. So what do you see?

Phil: Well, breath. That is what stands out in my mind at this point, but not a good portion of it, just a *lack* of. I have such a shortness of breath that I've never had before. Never. Meaning I feel as if, you know, I'm taking short breaths. I've smoked—I've freebased on occasion, it was like trying to get the smoke up into the chest. That's how I feel just walking occasionally sometimes. It's such…Yeah.

Dr. Miller: Yes?

Phil: …shortness of breath. I've never had that before either, but I most certainly do now.

Dr. Miller: Remember, I said the two ways, the two most common ways, to die from cocaine are shutdown of the respiratory system and cardiac arrest.

Phil: I've often felt that was so possible…It's amazing.

Dr. Miller: It does. The system shuts down—it almost feels like you're thick.…Ever had that feeling? You can't get some breath down, like the tube is shut off.

Phil: And yet, as bad as that gets, at least myself, and I don't know about everybody else, but you continue to do it! I mean, even at the point when there's no way that you can get any higher…

Dr. Miller: Say, "...no way *I* can get any higher."

Phil: ...No way, that *I* can get any higher, that's correct. And you continue—*I* continue to do it. That's what I can never understand....that I could *never* understand. Could not breathe any longer, couldn't even blow my nose, and continued to do it. Those are questions that I could never, never put an answer on. I don't even know if you can, Dr. Miller.

Dr. Miller: Well, Phil, I know this much. I know that if you hook a monkey up to a coke tube and every time he pulls a chain he receives some coke, he will keep pulling until he's dead. Even with food in the cage, even with a receptive female in the cage, the monkey will continue pulling the lever for the coke. He will not have sex with the female in the cage. The monkey will continue pulling the lever for the coke. He will not eat the food. He will just keep pulling the lever until he's dead. Now *that* I know. I know that cocaine is, if not *the, among* the most reinforcing of *all* drugs. *Reinforcing* means you get a reward every time you do something. If you put your hand out and you get a little piece of chocolate, you're liable to put your hand out again. You put your hand out again, you get another little piece of chocolate, and before you know it you might have a hand that's just always going out like this, because we like little pieces of chocolate reinforcing our behavior. Cocaine, like many other drugs, is a powerful reinforcer for human beings and for animals.

Phil: Well, here's an example of that. Where I live, freebasing is not extremely big. By that I mean I don't think any people are that aware or knowledgeable about it. Other parts of the state they are. So a friend of mine who had been doing it for some time (and I did it on occasion, three or four times in my life), but I think, I'd go out to see him. And I'd get there 5:00, and I'd say, Len, now let's go out for the evening, okay fine, we'll go out at 8:00. Well, now it'd be 8:00 and I'd say, "Let's get dressed," and he'd go, "Okay, we'll go out by 10:00 at the latest." Okay, well now it's quarter after twelve, and I'd say, "I'd like to go out tonight..." "We'll go to a great club at 1:00." Now it'd be a quarter after three, I'd be kicking the door down saying, "I'm leaving the place," he'd say, "I'll meet you for breakfast, no problem." Now, I'm just, to make a long story short, he felt that there was nothing better outside that room. That there was no sense to leave the room.

Dr. Miller: That's right.

Phil: So I saw him the following day at 4:30 after the Pitt/Notre Dame game, when he finally left the place. He was was supposed to meet me at the game. I mean, you know, not to criticize him in the least, just why should he go to the game? He had his own game there in his room with his drugs.

Dr. Miller: I want to emphasize that, while this connection to cocaine and other drugs is tough—it's beatable, and there are a lot of you out there who are beating it. I really don't believe that just sitting and talking and only doing a lot of verbal therapy, as good as it is, will do it. If I thought so, I would go back to a method that I've used a lot, which is having 24-hour-in-a-row or 48-hour-in-a-row verbal therapy sessions. They're called marathon group therapy sessions. This verbal stuff is important, but aerobic conditioning and nutritional training are also very important. This is because we're not made up of just the head, as much as we all like to be in our heads and talk and it's fun. We're not just a head. There are other parts that need to be taken care of. And they need a lot of care, and a lot of attention. It's just the name of the game, whether we want to do it or not. And you'll either attend to those parts, or they'll make sure you do, by doing something real severe and real dramatic. That's what some ulcers are about, that's what some headaches are about, that's what some backaches are about. Physical symptoms are messages calling for attention. Without getting esoteric about whether or not cancer is caused that way, we certainly know that ulcers and headaches and cardiovascular problems and so on have a lot to do with stress. And a lot of what stress has to do with is us living in our heads, and not taking the time to pay attention to messages from our feet, our backs, our necks or other areas in our bodies, and then doing something—to respond to the messages. Sometimes, responding to these body messages entails major lifestyle changes.

UNFINISHED BUSINESS EXERCISE

Unfinished business may be one of the greatest forces in history. So much remains unsaid, unexpressed, and then gets acted upon in convoluted ways. The unfinished business exercise taught below allows patients to express messages that may be locked inside, buried deep, but gnawing away at the personality. These messages may be positive, neutral, negative, and even suicidal. This is an especially valuable exercise for newcomers to group therapy, as are many people who enter addiction treatment, because it creates simple, nonthreatening ways of expressing and working with problems. Dr. Miller teaches this classic gestalt exercise and has his patients return to it frequently during the ongoing group therapy program. Patients tend to begin shyly, talking to people in the room and then progress to what you will read in Chapter 5, where Steve finally roars out his anger. In fact, experienced patients often get up and get themselves or someone else in the group an empty chair as a way of signaling the group that they are, or someone else is, ready "to work," to finish business with the person imagined to be sitting in the chair.

Dr. Miller: I encourage people to participate in an exercise called "Unfinished Business." Actually, we store much more than resents and appreciations in our unfinished business storage compartments, but those two are quite common.

Resentment is anger that's saved. Anger is like [bark!]. Something happens, and we have the basic, almost animal response of anger, and it comes right out. Anger of the moment is pretty clean. The other person can tell what it is. We express anger, and then we're done with it. The stuff that we save up for minutes, hours, days, weeks, months, even years—that's not clean anger anymore, it becomes resentment and hostility. It's the stuff we chew over and build up. We start to think about the other person or persons we are angry with and play and replay the scripts in our heads. These feelings weigh us down.

Appreciation can also weigh us down. Appreciation sounds like a nice thing to have around, but it's not. It's a fine thing to express. Yet if you don't express appreciation, it will eventually turn to resentment. It goes through various stages. If I have appreciation towards you and I don't express it, than I have it again and I don't express it, then after a while, I'm going to start to feel some sense of obligation, like a *should*. Like "I *ought* to do something—next time I see him, I *ought* to do something for him, I *ought* to call..." and the next thing I know, I'm carrying around this, this *stuff*, which began with appreciation. I wanted to tell you what a swell guy you are, how much I liked what you did for me that time. The next thing I know, I'm thinking, "I still haven't sent him a card, jerk!" and the next thing I'm calling *you* a jerk, and I'm resentful. What the hell, I want to thank him, I don't want to be around him, all I do when I'm around him is think about that time when I didn't thank him—I'm dramatizing the downside of carrying appreciation around.

So the game of resents and appreciations is to check yourself out, and just express—walk over to the person and express the resentment or appreciation. Or, you may not want to burden the other person, because it's yesterday's snow. I mean, suppose you have some resentment toward Leslie, that's three years old. What benefit is it to her for me to come over and unburden myself, by saying, "Hi there, I'm doing some kind of California experiment, I'm sharing my old resentment with you, aren't you delighted?" Who needs to hear that? If it is three years old, it is *my* problem. You don't have to hear it.

The same is true for appreciation. Possibly, if I still have clean appreciation, I could say to you, "You know, you did this for me three years ago, and I never mentioned my appreciation." This might not be a burden, you might enjoy hearing the appreciation, but you certainly do not enjoy sharing my resentment.

Now I can explain to you all the reason I have an empty chair in the center of the circle. The empty chair is a tool for what we call *psychodrama*—a way in which I can unload myself, unburden myself, of stuff that I'm carrying around, without having to inflict it on the person toward whom it was originally aimed. The empty chair is a way to get out—to express—this stale, unexpressed material that I'm carrying around. I can do it without having to burden the person, whoever it is directed toward. When you use this empty chair, I will sometimes ask you to switch over and be the other person. You will then actually get into the chair. This is a way of getting into both sides of what the internal voices in the repressed or suppressed script are saying. Usually, when we don't express something, it is because we have some anticipation of what the other person will do in response, and we don't want to face that. We don't want to hear what they have to say. So we end up carrying what we have to say around in the form of unfinished business.

We have the capacity to take these thoughts of unfinished business, and create emotions. I can go into my room, close the door, pull the drapes, maybe even get into the closet, and think up some very uncomfortable thing that happened to me or is going to happen to me, and make myself feel real tight, uncomfortable, threatened, quivering, crying.

One of you has discussed spite with me. Spite is a very dangerous form of unfinished business. The extreme of spite is suicide. I'll kill myself, and when you see the blood on the floor and you see my laying there dead, you'll feel like shit!"

Susan: That's right. That's certainly right.

Dr. Miller: That's what suicide is often about.

Susan: Don't dare me to do anything!

Dr. Miller: Suicide is me turning in on myself as a way to get at you.

Susan: That's right.

Dr. Miller: And the way out of that is to express directly, "You sonofabitch, I wanna make you feel bad! And I'm gonna make you feel bad by pointing my finger at you and telling you what a shit you are!" You see how that's the opposite of "I'm gonna make myself feel so bad, you can't stand to look at me feeling so bad, and you'll feel terrible."

Susan: Got it.

Dr. Miller: Another manifestation of unfinished business is catastrophizing. Say, for example, you are worrying about an IRS audit and you can't find your files for the years they're auditing. You say to yourself, "Do I bring in '79 and '80 and '82 as a way to show them that I'm a good boy and I save all my files and I just happened to lose '81? Or do I not bring in anything, and I just say to them, "I lost '81"? Or do I make up some lie and I say, "Somebody came into my house and they stole '81"? [Laughter.]

Susan: We'd've helped.

Dr. Miller: You fear the worst, despite the route you take. These are catastrophic expectations. You think of the worst thing that can happen. But that thought doesn't help you find the files. It doesn't change the reality of whether they're missing or not. It doesn't really change whatever will happen to you. It is simply one thought out of thousands, one which you choose to have as a way of punishing yourself. The trick with those catastrophic expectations is to watch them. Be able to notice what you are doing to yourself, rather than be so involved with catastrophizing that you can't do anything about it. Make yourself feel good by a mechanical means, by deep breathing, for example.

So. Resents and appreciations. If you have them toward anyone in the room, toward the building, toward the wood pile, toward a person who's not here, speak up.

Take the risk here: Try out something different by expressing the resent or the appreciation. Or, if you don't want to do that here, say it out loud when you're alone: listen to your tone of voice and really get the feeling out.

Tom: Can I express my appreciation now?

Dr. Miller: Sure! Select a person in this room, or put someone from outside in the empty chair.

Tom: I was leading up to something, but I do want to express my appreciation to Jim. First of all, I want to say that—but see, I'm always concerned that I'm too maudlin.

Dr. Miller: Okay, so there's a voice in you, even as you're talking, saying, "Watch out, Tom, you're liable to be too maudlin."

Tom: No, I guess I mean I'm too soft.

Dr. Miller: Too what? Too soft? Okay, so we have two parts of you now to polish up. The part of you that's saying you're too maudlin, and the part of you that's saying you're too soft. So say what you're gonna say now, and purposely be real soft and maudlin.

[Laughter.]

Tom: Purposely say I'm appreciative in a soft and maudlin way?

Dr. Miller: Purposely! See, that's how you bring a habit to awareness. By purposely doing it. You do it again and again and again, and then awareness grows. For example, if I want to be in touch with my posture, this bending forward that I do, the way to teach myself and to raise my awareness, is to purposely slouch, even exaggerate my slouch. I get the feel of what the slouch really is doing to my body. Now, Tom, purposely be maudlin or very soft, or both. And get a feel for what it is that you're criticizing in yourself as you do this.

Tom: Well, first I wanna say that, uh, when I came here on Sunday night I was really very angry. When I came into this room, I was really angry and upset. Nothing about this program made sense to me, especially group therapy. But my resentment has led to a genuine affection, and I'm very happy that everyone is here. And then I appreciate everybody in the room, because there's not one of you, whether it be, uh...(I'm not *trying to be maudlin, now, see, I'm just trying to say what I'm going to say, but I'm being maudlin...*).

Susan: Continue!

Tom: I don't even know what the term *maudlin* means!

Dr. Miller: Are you feeling that you're getting maudlin?

Susan: Does *maudlin* mean gooshy?

Frank: Yeah.

Dr. Miller: Well, let's find out what he means specifically. We don't really know. We might guess what he means by what we each mean by too maudlin.

Tom: There hasn't been one individual here, unequivocally, that has not extended a kindness or an overture, that has not been very, very deeply appreciated, and I want to thank you all for everything. I'm feeling very frightened about leaving my sanctuary here. 'Cause I don't feel ready to go back to face what I have to face. I'm going—my life is very tumultuous. My business is very tumultuous, and I wouldn't give it up in a second. But I sometimes think that I'd probably be better off being a poet, and or a musician, and listening to beautiful music, and sitting by water, and the music and the water that really give me great tranquility, but yet, there's that excitement in my business that I wouldn't give up for the world. And then there's some days when I just can't get all my priorities in order. And I don't know how I'm ever going to deal with my priorities. My demands in life. It frightens me.

Dr. Miller: Say, "I frighten myself." It doesn't frighten you, you do.

Tom: I frighten myself, because I think my priorities have gotten so excessive. Maybe I'm my drinking, or with the cocaine, because I really can't deal with my life adequately. I'm not suggesting that I'm spiteful or suicidal, and I would never want to be suicidal. I feel I have too much to live for, but I just don't know if I'll ever adequately be able to enjoy my life nearly to the fullest, because I'm filled with so much anxiety and worry...I'm just very worried about everything.

SEMANTIC AWARENESS EXERCISE

The semantic awareness exercise is also adapted from the gestalt approach. As is the case for any form of increased awareness, semantic awareness must be developed through practice. Semantic awareness exercises encourage a closer awareness of word choice in order to better hear the feelings and messages behind the words. In this section, Dr. Miller is teaching one form of semantic awareness by examining the use of words such as "why."

Susan: I have a question. [Laughter.] How come I come into group (and this has happened to me when I was in group therapy before), how come, as soon as I come into a group situation....

Dr. Miller: You get tired?

Susan: I get tired. [Laughter.] I don't like it at all. It's very, very frustrating, extremely so. And I went through eleven years worth of therapy, in group, and every single solitary time, I used to get myself totally into a trance, when, I mean, y'all could function, y'all could do everything, and it looks like I was with you, but I was just in another world. And I find myself doing that every time I walk in this room. And it's making me angry at myself, and I don't...I mean, what is it? I mean, why is it?

Dr. Miller: What are you doing to make yourself tired? You're withdrawing rather than participating.

Susan: Well, *why* do I do that?

Dr. Miller: I don't answer that question.

Susan: You're a lot of help!

Dr. Miller: I will answer the question if you'll turn it into a *how* question.

Susan: Okay. How come I do this?

Dr. Miller: *How come* is *why*. [Laughter.] There's a difference between *why* and *how*. *How come* and *why* are exactly the same.

Susan: Okay. But could you explain more?

Dr. Miller: The *why* question is a self-accusation. You're saying, "Why do I get tired?" And what's behind that question, is "What's wrong with me that I get tired?" and what's behind that question is a statement, which is, "There must be something wrong with me that I get tired continuously in groups." *Why* questions, toward ourselves and toward other people, are frequently disguised accusations. They are one of the ways that we make ourselves feel terrible. *How come* is a disguised *why* question. And if you look carefully behind every *why* question, interpersonal (I'm not talking abut scientific *why* questions, that's another whole area), but interpersonal *why* questions, if you look behind them, you will find an imbedded accusation. And there is no way you can answer an accusation that either comes from another person or comes from yourself. All you're doing is making yourself feel bad. Because the accusation that's hidden behind the *why* question is: "You must be sick/bad/crazy or stupid, because if you weren't either sick or bad or crazy or stupid, you wouldn't be getting tired in group again and again."

Susan: But I do not believe that. I do not believe that. I just don't buy it.

Dr. Miller: You don't buy what?

Susan: That I have to be one of those because that's why I get tired in group.

Dr. Miller: No, but that's what you may be saying to yourself. The accusation is "Why am I getting tired?" "…because if I weren't sick, bad, crazy or stupid, I wouldn't be getting tired."

Susan: I just know I don't like it.

Dr. Miller: You don't like *it*. And the *it* in that sentence is *Susan*. And what you're saying is, "I don't like myself."

Susan: All right. I do not like myself. But that does not change the fact that I keep tuning out and almost putting myself in a self-hypnotic trance. I do not want to do this, and I need to know how to not do this.

Dr. Miller: Yes. The *how* question. How to change. That's a useful question.

Susan: Okay.

Dr. Miller: See, that'll tell you something to do. The *why* is an accusation. It's looking for an intellectual answer. But it won't tell you what to do. It will send you in circles instead.

Susan: I mean, this group therapy is the most valuable time that we have, and I…whatever, retreat, run, get sleepy.

Dr. Miller: So how can you stay awake?

Susan: Cocaine. [Laughter.] I did not mean that.…

Dr. Miller: Mmmm, hmmm hmmm, hmmm. Cocaine.…

Susan: I never use cocaine to stay awake.

Dr. Miller: How else can you stay awake?

Susan: I don't know.

Dr. Miller: You do.

Susan: I do?

Dr. Miller: Tell me three things you can do to stay awake—are you sleeping right now?

Susan: No.

Dr. Miller: No. So one thing you can do is to speak up.

Susan: Oh.…

Dr. Miller: Which means get involved in the group rather than withdraw from it. Which I think is related to your entire life. To get involved with your life rather than withdraw into a room with a base pipe. Okay, what's another thing you can do to stay awake here?

Susan: I don't know…I moved…I'm withdrawing again.

Jackie: Are you sleeping right now?

Susan: No, it's, I don't know, but I can just feel myself withdrawing.

Dr. Miller: Right now.

Susan: Right now. Right this second. Because I was not tired when I walked through that door. I was not sleepy when I walked through that door. I was wide awake. And I've watched this happen every time I come in this room. And I do not like it at all. I mean...it's not what's good for me, and I just...I mean, I can't sit here and talk the whole time we're in group, to keep awake. I almost asked another *why* question.

Dr. Miller: Okay, ask it. You're not going to stop them right away. The thing to do is to continue asking them, but then point out to yourself that you're criticizing yourself.

Susan: Well, if I do not want to withdraw, then why am I withdrawing? Because I do not want to withdraw. I mean, there's no reason. In the groups I've been in before, there was a reason. I didn't like any of them. I mean, it was a total bore. I mean, I went to sleep in group, because I was there because I had to be there. Because if I didn't go, my therapist would come pick me up and take me there anyway. So I was there by force. So I just got there, and I'd look at the floor, and finally I'd get myself all glassy-eyed, and I was in my little world—my own world. I can just turn me off just like a radio, but I can't always turn me back on.

Dr. Miller: Wow.

Susan: But I don't want to do that here, and it's really frustrating me.

Dr. Miller: So perhaps you have a habit. A conditioned response to group therapy. As soon as you walk into this group, all that old feeling about group turns on inside you and you just withdraw. After eleven years of walking into a room and tuning out—going to sleep, it must be a little difficult to go into a room and stay awake.

Susan: That makes sense.

Dr. Miller: Yes! You've got an old habit.

Susan: But I haven't been in group now for years. You mean the old habit's back, huh?

Dr. Miller: That's one thing. I don't think it's as simple as that, but that could be one explanation. Another one is being involved rather than withdrawing.

Susan: I mean, I am very, very concerned with what everyone here has to say.

Dr. Miller: Tell Lou Ann something you've been afraid to tell her.

Susan: I already told her last night. [Laughing.]

Dr. Miller: Do you have anything that you haven't told...anybody?

Lou Ann: What did you tell me last night?

Dr. Miller: Any withholds?

Susan: I told you how much I was relating to you last night.

Dr. Miller: Look around the room. Who do you have a withhold toward?

Susan: No one.

Dr. Miller: Not one drop? You've been totally honest? Do you look around the room that quickly? There's not one person that you've been "not saying" something to? Withholds are another thing that tire us out. If I go into a room, and there are a lot of things that I want to say, and I'm holding back, that will make me tired, because the energy of holding back all that stuff is tiring. So what did you find when you looked around the room?

Susan: I can't say.

Dr. Miller: Say, "I won't say."

Susan: I won't say.

Dr. Miller: Say, "I refuse to say."

Susan: I refuse to say.

Dr. Miller: Say, "I'd rather use the energy to hold all that stuff in."

Susan: No, that's not the case. I just…[Laughter.] That is absolutely not the case.

Dr. Miller: Oh no? That's what you're doing.

Susan: Why don't we change the subject.

Dr. Miller: Sure! Take a little nap, I'll go on.

Susan: I don't *want* to take a nap! *I want to be conscious!* Okay? So next time I start feeling sleepy, can I get up? I mean, can I walk around a little bit?

Dr. Miller: Absolutely! Sure! Oh, so you have another method. Walk over to the sink , put water on your face, jump up and down, make some noise….Definitely!

Susan: Okay. 'Cause I do not want to go to sleep. This is too valuable of a time. And I'll be cheating myself if I do that.

Dr. Miller: Okay. Let's get back to the *why* question. It's a very important tool, the understanding of the *why* question. The classic *why* question is the parent saying to the child, "Why did you spill that milk?" And the child looks up and hears this voice of accusation, with the question, "Why did you spill that milk?" And the child tries to answer the question, "*Why* did I spill that milk?" I mean, "Why *did* I spill that milk?" I mean, there's this adult asking me the question, "Why did I spill the milk?" so there must be an answer to it. What is the answer? And yet the child can't come up with an answer, because there is often no answer to an accusation.

So the child is getting a double message. The music—the *sound* of the question—is accusatory: "mmm-mm-mmm-mmm-mmm"! The lyrics— the words—are a question. And there we have the beginning of crazy-making. Because the child wonders, "What's wrong with me that I can't answer the question?" (*Why* can't I…) "I must be incompetent! Because otherwise, if I were competent, I'd be able to answer the question."

Of course, the child isn't thinking in those words. But that's the basic message. After all, if the parent asked the question, there must be an answer to it. If the little boy doesn't have an answer, there must be something wrong with him. He thinks, "Now there's *two* things wrong with me. One is that I spilled the milk, and the other is that I can't answer the question about why I spilled it." And this is the beginning of the self-imposed crazy-making that we all do to ourselves.

Behind the parent's question of "Why did you spill the milk?" is a very simple statement: "Rrrrowrrrrrh!!!! I'm angry at you! You inconvenienced me! *I've* got to clean up the milk! *You* don't!" That's the statement behind the question. The parent doesn't really want or expect the child to give a discourse on why he spilled the milk. Whoever expects an answer to a question like "Why did you spill the milk?" or "Why did you chip my best plate? Can you give me three reasons why you chipped my best plate?" But what's behind the question, "Damn! I am angry that you chipped my plate! I liked that plate." That you don't have to answer. There is no answer to the direct expression of annoyance or anger. There's no answer called for. It's "Oh damn, that milk, right on my rug. Oh shit!" and I clean it up, and that's it. And the kid doesn't have to be figuring out…the kid feels the anger, but doesn't have to be figuring it out, "What's *wrong with me* that I did this?"

Why questions call for a defense at minimum. And they're an unfair accusation at maximum. Any time….Why are you sitting like that, Diane? See, it's calling for you to explain. There must be something wrong with you. And then, sometimes, the music to the why question can sound very nice. It can be a very friendly *why* question. Oh, by the way, Jack, why are you sitting with your hand in between your legs like that? You see, so the music in that one is not offensive, but the question still calls for an explanation, puts Jack on the defensive; he has to explain to me why his hand is in between his legs. He's not on this earth to explain his posture to anybody. Why is your car parked the wrong way…why are you wearing a…? See, each of these questions, *why* questions, calls for a defensive explanation of your behavior. So, if you try to take on that question, you're on the defensive. There's an accusation behind it. And whenever you're not sure of that, just think of the one with the child. 'Cause what we do to ourselves when we ask ourselves these *why* questions is we begin what's called a *spiral mind molestation*.

One thing we try to do is we try to figure out why we take drugs. "Why do I take coke? I mean, why *do* I take coke? I mean, if there wasn't something wrong with me, I wouldn't continue to take coke. I mean, I'd probably just take a little…I mean, why can't I control the coke at least? I mean, that's the issue. I mean, I could take some coke, but why can't I control the coke and just take a little amount? There must be something wrong. I mean, I must have…maybe I'm trying to cover something up. I mean, I wouldn't be thinking this way if there wasn't something underneath that made me think this way.…" You see how the spiral begins? "Why am I doing this to myself? Why do I continue to do this to myself? I wake up in the morning and I feel so bad, and I tell myself I'm not gonna do it again, and then I do it…why *am* I doing that? And we go around with these *why* questions until we feel worse and worse and worse.

Now, if you want to question yourself, with regard to cocaine or other things that you're doing, a much more productive question is the *how* question. 'Cause the *why* question is an accusation or calls for a defense, whereas the *how* question gives you the mechanism. *How* is mechanistic. How do I put on my shoes? I reach out, I take a shoe, I pick it up, I pull it on. How do I make my eggs? I take my eggs…You see, it tells you each of the mechanisms. How do I get my coke? rather than *why* do I get my coke? How do I get my coke? [To Susan]: Come on back, now's the time to jump up. Come on, come on, jump around, jump around, come on, you said you were gonna walk! I saw you drifting, Susan. [Laughter.]

Now that's one thing you can do as a *how*. How can you stay awake? You can ask the people next to you for a little help. You can say, "Hey, if you see me drifting off, poke me, will ya? I've got an old habit of sleeping in group." [Laughter as someone pokes her.] There!

Tom: I'll keep her awake!

Dr. Miller: See—*how* do I get my coke? I have this urge for coke. I reach out for the telephone. I pick the phone receiver off the hook and pull it toward me—this is how. I think of the telephone number. I call my dealer. Or—how do I get my coke? I go and get my car keys. Now I'm walking down the stairs. Now I'm opening up the door. If you pay attention like this to the steps, at any moment, at any second really, as you're making those little choices, you can say, "Hey, I'm reaching for my car keys. I'm on my way to the door. This is how I'm gonna get my coke. I can decide to put the car keys down and go sit in my chair and look at how I'm feeling the craving." Rather than this automatic, this conditioned behavior, which is just grab the car keys, go for the door, in the car, down the road, toward the deal, before you even think about it. In fact, all the way there, you might even be asking yourself, "Why am I doing this? Why am I doing this? Why am I doing this? And not once looking at "How am I doing this? I'm driving the car, I got my foot on the gas. I can turn the car around and go home." But we can *why*-question ourselves all the way to the dealer: "Why am I here now? Why am I buying this much? I don't need this much!" *Why* questions are not effective tools. Take careful notes on how you talk to yourself. The words you select tell you something.

So look at the *how* of your behavior. "How am I sitting like this?" rather than "Why am I sitting like this?" How? I've got my body leaning over to the left-hand side, I've got my hand out, I can put my back up straight and sit up straight. The *how* is the mechanism. And that's what you ought to be in touch with. And watch out for the *how come?* because *how come?* is *why?* And that again is just going to give you this, this sort of intellectual defensive rationalization. "How come I keep doing cocaine? How come I'm interested in a glass of champagne?" And then you start spiraling to try to answer it. "How am I reaching for champagne? I'm putting my arm out and I'm reaching towards the glass. How do I stop? Drop the glass." Any questions on this *why* question tool? This is a very valuable tool, and I hope you can assimilate it. And if you don't, let's bring it up again later tonight. Because it's one of the most common ways that we drive ourselves crazy, that we make ourselves feel bad.

With this spiraling of the *why* question, we create tension in our bodies. Rather than looking at "How am I making my stomach tight? I ask, "Why am I making my stomach tight?" The *how* is simple. "How am I making my stomach tight? I'm holding my breath in, pushing on the muscles, while I talk. How do I make my stomach loose? Stop holding my breath, and breathe and move the muscles." That's the mechanism. "How am I making...?" Why am I making my stomach tight? I could be sitting here and asking myself why I'm making my stomach tight for the next half hour, and never take the time to loosen the muscles. Just keep asking this over and over, "Why am I doing this, what's wrong with me? Why am I doing this again? I still have this tight feeling in my stomach?" All the time I'm doing that, I'm holding the muscles tight and I'm not breathing. I think some of you saw this demonstrated very graphically last night. Occasionally I'd say to one of you, "Breathe," and you'd hear that person breathe and go [sighing sound], and prior to my saying that, the person was holding his or her breath. A few people were crying, and then just right in the middle of crying, I could see that there was no breathing going on. Which means the opposite of what was necessary was happening. [To Susan.] Jump around! Jump around! Stay with us! [Laughter.] Yeah, poke her with the stick! Gently, please.

Tom: Dr. Miller

Dr. Miller: Yes.

Tom: Uh, just as you're telling me this, I was just reflecting on me last night, when I started getting tied up in the *why*, I became repressive and withdrew into myself.

Dr. Miller: Yes.

Tom: And just started going, spiraling down.

Dr. Miller: Spiraling down.

Tom: Rapidly. And I realized it, but without a lot of, without the cognizance of what you're telling me now, I got up out of there because I stopped asking *why?* and started asking *how?* And then, when I woke up this morning, I found a bunch of other *how*s and those *how*s solved, or got me out of that spiral.

Dr. Miller: Mmm-hmm. Methods, methods. Tools.

Tom: That's exactly, exactly what has been my demesis. Nemesis.

Dr. Miller: Yeah, demesis. Demise.

Tom: Yes, right.

Dr. Miller: That was a good slip. Yes, Phil?

Phil: We're so mind oriented that we're always looking for the *why*, the *why* question comes out of our conditioning, our intellectual conditioning, the thinking rather than the feeling, or being aware of. And all through this week what we're learning is to be aware.

Dr. Miller: So the *how* leads to awareness, the *why* leads to thinking, the intellectualizing. Asking *how* may raise awareness of the mechanism or method, whereas asking *why* leads to defensiveness.

"Why do I get so tired in group therapy?"

5

Undrugging the Feelings

But I probably only need
The love of human touch
What a simple cure
For such a deadly disease
Sometimes just a big hug
Will put me at ease.

(Anonymous Group Therapy Participant)

Group therapy patients share their experiences and their feelings and discover that they are not alone. They also learn to listen to themselves and to each other—to dissect their problems into manageable parts.

Persons who are addicted to drugs have made a habit of burying their feelings—of substituting the chemical roller coaster ride for the ups and downs of real life. For many of the participants in these group therapy sessions, just talking about feelings is a new, or a newly revived, experience. As a person emerges from the haze of drug addiction, he or she is barraged by a stream of long-overlooked sensation and emotion. All too often, the simplest of expressions about the simplest of these feelings is a challenge. Feeling real feelings, whether positive or negative or neutral, and then talking about them is a skill that may have to be relearned, or learned for the first time, by a patient who has spent years under the influence of drugs.

BREAKING THROUGH DECEITS

Tangled in the mesh of the addicted person's unexpressed feelings is an elaborate denial system. Large and small lies are stored. The lies trigger long chains of deceitful behavior. Others and oneself are deceived. Beginning to talk about even small deceits is an important part of opening up in this form of group therapy. Here, we see how the awareness exercise leads to such a discussion.

Dr. Miller: Tom what are you most aware of at this second?

Tom: My stomach. Garlic dinner. Mike's cooking [laughing].

Dr. Miller: Okay, what's the second thing you're most aware of in your body?

Tom: I'm not quite sure. I have a feeling inside of my body I can't quite...

Dr. Miller: What's the next thing you notice?

Tom: Feeling touched by listening to Susan.

Dr. Miller: I think you all may be making the exercise more difficult than it is. When I say, "What are you most aware of?" what you might be most aware of is your hands touching each other. You might be most aware of a pressure on your leg. Some underwear that's tight. Whatever it is, it's some awareness. There's no right or wrong in the exercise. Now, what are you the most aware of, Tom?

Tom: Sitting on a cushion for the first time. [Laughter.] Not sitting on the hard chair.

Dr. Miller: What are you most aware of, Tom?

Tom: I'm most aware that the fact that I'm feeling very, very, I have such a very strong feelings about some of the people in the room....

Dr. Miller: Can you tell them?

Tom: I think you're delicious. [Laughter.]

Mike: I've been called a lot of things, but I've never been called delicious.

Mark: I bet you have!

Mike: I'll have to look that one up in Webster, to see if there's....

Mark: I'll define it for you.

Tom: You are a really unique individual. And if you only knew how wonderful you were, and if you just wouldn't be so hard on yourself, you're really great, you're really quite unique. Very special. I can't stand that fact that you're just—you really—you seem to be in such pain, so hard on yourself. And it really bothers me.

Mark: I'll second those feelings.

Dave: Me, too. It's hard for me to see you do that. It's just hard for me to be quiet. It's hard for me not to say anything. It's hard for me to sit here and watch you do that.

Tom: I'm aware of the fact that I'm very, very thankful that you're not feeling too badly about me.

Dr. Miller: Getting maudlin again?

Mike: Why don't you tell the group? Tell the group. About Laura.

Tom: I don't know if the doctor can take it...!

Mike: Oh, I don't know, I think he can! If Laura can take it, he can take it.

Tom: Well, I didn't particularly care for the exercise class. It wasn't particularly appealing to me, but I knew that there was going to be a class at 2:10, and...

Dr. Miller: When was that?

Tom: The other day.

Dr. Miller: Oh, the other day.

Tom: ...and I just fibbed a little bit about the time. Laura asked what time it was, and I said, it was 3:10, it was really ten after two!

Frank: You set your watch ahead too, didn't you? [Laughter.]

Mike: That's not the end of it!

Tom: No, that's it. That's the end of it!

Mike: Well, then you went in and....

Tom: Oh, well, then I had, then I wanted to be sure that Laura knew what the real time was, so I went into this long spiel with Gail, "What time do you have?" So anyway, I felt kind of guilty about that, because it was really kind of, it was very deceitful.

Frank: Sleaze ball.

Tom: Sleaze ball.

Mike: Don't you love it? Isn't it great? Terrific? I knew he'd love it!

Dr. Miller: [Laughing.] Talk about delicious! [Laughter.]

Tom: And then I was, I was very very appreciative of Laura, she was very attentive, to notice last night that I wasn't quite, I wasn't quite satisfied with....You know, I went off, I go off on tangents, that's a problem of mine, sometimes I do it intentionally, sometimes I don't, and that very often...I mean, I was the one that initiated trying to cut the whole session with me short last night, and then when it was cut, I sort of like felt like my problems weren't resolved. So I felt like lost. So Laura noticed that, and she was very, it was sweet of her. But I didn't say so.

Mike: I noticed that, too. We went around the room and said we thought that you were important enough to take up our time, and then we switched the subject. And I thought, I thought to myself, "Wait a minute. He probably still has more to say!"

Tom: I did. I—I felt cheated, even though I wanted not—I wanted it to end, and then when it did, I felt cheated.

Dr. Miller: Good. Because you cheated yourself.

Tom: And then I was sorry that I did.

Dr. Miller: Yes. So you learned something. You learned about deceiving yourself and others, even in small ways. It cheats you. You cheat you.

IDENTIFYING AND CONNECTING CRAVINGS

When staying off drugs is the goal, a new response to cravings for drugs must be developed. While other addiction therapies attempt to get rid of cravings, Dr. Miller embraces cravings as simply another feeling to be experienced. Being able to fully experience a craving without responding with use takes a high level of self-awareness and self-control. Below, Dr. Miller helps a group member focus in on the experience of craving. Giving the craving a hypothetical place in the body is a step toward gestalting. Dr. Miller also explains the dangerous relationship between cravings for different drugs.

Tom: Mmm-hmmm. And then, also, uh, I'm thankful to David for telling me, explaining to me that I was an alcoholic. Because I really didn't know. I—I—I always thought that an alcoholic, really, was somebody that was really rip-roaring drunk all the time.

Mark: Oh. Uh-huh.

Tom: And he has a definition about alcoholics, I'm an alcoholic, so I really was very confused about that. I wasn't trying to rationalize...I wasn't really sure. I think from the very beginning, I was honest about that. And I was, then on Sunday—when was Zeke here? It was either Sunday or Monday....

Dr. Miller: Zeke was here on Sunday.

Tom: And he immediately had the feeling that I was an alcoholic.

Dr. Miller: You were. Yeah.

Tom: But I didn't think he was necessarily right, yet I wasn't sure.

Dr. Miller: Sometimes it takes two alcoholics to convince a third one. [Laughter.]

Tom: Well, no, but I—the definition of *alcoholic*—he really didn't define that.

Dr. Miller: How did he make it palatable?

Tom: He's the same kind of an alcoholic…

Dr. Miller: Yes.

Tom: …you know, *was* the same kind of an alcoholic.

Dr. Miller: So what did David say to you to make it acceptable to you, or that allowed your awareness to say, "Yes, this is what I do also"?

Tom: Well, he explained the habit that he had, and how he learned that he was an alcoholic. And then I believe what he says to me, he says, "That's alcoholism," he learned that that's alcoholism, so I believe that I'm an alcoholic.

Dr. Miller: And what is it that he did when he drank that you understand?

Tom: He used to drink—it was very, very important to him to have those couple of drinks. It was more important than going to bed with his wife.…I would go down and want those couple of drinks, the way I wanted the cocaine. Uh, so if I wanted that.…

Dr. Miller: You could feel that. As soon as he said it, you knew what he was talking about.

Tom: Oh, 'cause I would wanna go down and have those—I would make an excuse to my wife, "Oh, I gotta go down and do something…" and I'd go down and have a couple of drinks and snort my cocaine.

Dr. Miller: Good for you. I could sense it, the way you talked about that "civilized glass of champagne." There's a quality that's different.

Tom: Also that taste for that champagne didn't leave me from the moment that it came to mind—I wanted that glass of liquor, or whatever—it really didn't have to be champagne, I would settle for maybe, you know, a glass of beer, and I don't even like beer that much. But I wanted a drink this afternoon. And I was very uncomfortable sitting here; all I could think about was the drink.

Dr. Miller: Mmm-hmm. Can you locate that feeling in your body? Where is the craving: Or is it mostly in your head? Or everywhere? The feeling from the drink?

Tom: Can I pinpoint the location?

Dr. Miller: Yes. From what part of the body does the feeling come?

Tom: My tongue.

Dr. Miller: Good. Good for you!

Tom: Just the taste.

Dr. Miller: What you can do, Tom, now that you've got the location of your feeling, is play with it. You can make it a point of interest. You can make it a point of play, you can make it a point of intellectual curiosity—you can do lots of different things with the area without having to be compelled to drink. Because you've got in-between steps. See, without identifying the feeling, you have only a generalized feeling, you call

"Drink," and you just start reaching, without even being aware of where the feeling comes from.

Tom: But what you're suggesting then is when I have the craving—the urge for drink…

Dr. Miller: Go right into it. Don't try to ignore the craving. Accept it. Don't try to fight it. Play with it. Look at it. Say, "Oh, yeah, this is part of my craving. This part of my, my connection with alcohol."

Tom: Do I substitute that craving with something?

Dr. Miller: What would you like?

Tom: Well….

Dr. Miller: A glass of water? Go right ahead.

Tom: Do I…? Is that the best thing to do? Or do I sit with that craving and realize I have the craving?

Dr. Miller: There isn't a best. There are a lot of things to do. What I'm suggesting to all of you is not to fight your craving. You're not going to stop thinking of a blue canary if somebody says, "Stop thinking of a blue canary." Try not to think of a blue canary right now. No matter what you do, don't think of a blue canary. You can do anything else, but push blue canaries out of your head. You see, you have to think of the blue canary in order to push it out of your head, and then you're thinking about the blue canary. Accept the craving is going to come. Play with it. Look at it. See if you can spread it. See if you can feel a craving for alcohol with every cell in your body. While you're looking at it, say, "This is what my craving is. I now crave alcohol with every cell in my body." I'm not suggesting doing this in your office, necessarily. You might want to do this in the privacy of your home, or even your garage. Maybe you'll want to scream out loud for alcohol. With all your heart. Scream. Give it expression. Don't try to stuff it back in. Give it expression. But an expression other than drinking.

Tom: I had given up smoking for 3-1/2 years. And…but I went back, uh, about a year ago.

Dr. Miller: I noticed. Remember? I took the cigarettes out of your hand. I could feel that. I thought maybe they were satisfying something so strong that we'd get to something deeper by your not having the crutch in your hand.

Tom: And I'm bringing this up because I'm concerned with repressing my desire for alcohol and for cocaine, because I thought I would never smoke again. And then I did.

Dr. Miller: I hope you understand that, with regard to cocaine and alcohol, you can have that same kind of resolve, you can have that length of time off the habit, and you can go back to it. And there's a powerful connection between your cocaine use, alcohol use, and your cigarette use.

Tom: It's the connection between the three now.

Dr. Miller: Yes!

Tom: The cocaine and the liquor and the cigarettes.

Dr. Miller: Yes! Yes!

Tom: Thank God there's nothing else! [Laughter.]

Dr. Miller: But there is! You'll find it!

Tom: Although I do get a great joy out of going into a drugstore and looking at the pills.

Dr. Miller: Looking at what? At the pills! Well, that may be your next thing to watch out for; you can save yourself a step. I'm serious!

Tom: No, I haven't been addicted to any pills.

Dr. Miller: I don't think you have, but that could be your next addiction. That's the warning that you're coming out with. Now, pills don't fit your image of glamour. The other three do. You hear that in your language as well? There's something about the glamour—you're in Hollywood. It's hard not to be touched by that. I understand that. So you've got this picture of yourself, beautifully dressed, snorting a little coke, sipping a little champagne, with a beautiful cigarette in your hand!

Mark: Listening to the opera!

Dr. Miller: Ah, yes, listening to the opera!

Tom: Dahling…!

Dr. Miller: Okay. You'll be our David Niven.

[Group laughter.]

Dr. Miller: You're responding to image making, and you know that, and you make the images. You're in the business that makes the images. You've bought in. I mean, what's really so glamorous about licking an ashtray? Or smelling like a brewery?

GIVING FULL VOICE TO BURIED FEELINGS

Expressing oneself to the fullest is essential in the healing of pent-up hurts and old wounds. Anything that sits inside unexpressed can rear its ugly head and call back old patterns of drugging feelings and other forms of self-abuse. Full expression of feelings on a regular basis helps to avoid the build-up of old, unexpressed hurt, anger, resentment, etc. This way there is no dangerous storage of new but unexpressed wounds— wounds that will fester if not disinfected via expression.

The making of sounds that go with feelings—such as the sound of one's anger—is classic gestalt. This is an important technique for addiction-focused psychotherapy participants. They first learn to use it in group and then take it home as a personal tool. In the following section, Dr. Miller works with some particularly painful buried feelings.

Note his sensitivity to the patient's readiness, and careful timing. Follow his careful encouragement of Steve in the process of giving full voice to unexpressed feelings. This is one of my favorite passages. The emergence of the raw emotion has a powerful effect on everyone who hears it. This is human energy seeking—craving—expression, and, through expression, resolution.

Laura: Steve. Maybe you could share with the group some of the feelings that you've been having today.

Steve: Okay. I—uh—crashed last night. Emotionally crashed. From empathy. From Laura. I was ready to leave. And I didn't. There's too much love here for me to leave. That's not the answer. And the answer of leaving was leaving life, so that wasn't the answer. So, uh, I tried to stay up and reflect on all of this. 'Cause I felt very lonely, too, and I knew that I had been supersensitive about rejection, and it was growing on me, and I got myself into a bind. Got myself looking at this unknown terrible fear within me. And I just—tried to split. Couldn't handle it. And so I went down and smoked about sixteen cigarettes around midnight, 1:00 in the morning, by myself…I was trying to reflect and introspect and to understand this. And I couldn't do it. This is the second time I've crashed here. So I'm beginning to understand what Dr. Miller is talking about, about process. I've begun the process of unwinding the tangle of what has always scared me. And what it is is that I've been denying myself. I've been denying who I am. That I didn't *know* who I was, and I don't know totally who I am, and I will never know totally who I am, 'cause I'm always changing and growing and learning. And so I can't lie down and be stagnant—that would be great, to just lie down and be stagnant, I wouldn't have to learn anymore, and I could get all caught up, and then I'd be a rock, but I'm always seeking and learning, so I'm always going to have this experience. But nevertheless…boy, it's difficult to explain, I understand it within myself, and I hope I can explain it to you. Uh…I've had a rough childhood—not rough compared to some of you, but the only one I knew was mine, so it seemed pretty rough to me.…

Dr. Miller: Say a few things that were rough about your childhood.

Steve: Well, uh, my father's an alcoholic, and used to drink hard whiskey, and it made him real mean, very mean, and this was when I was maybe fifteen. Hurt me a lot to see him be that mean toward my mother, and indifferent toward my brother and me. And, uh, I guess some trauma happened between my mother and father, and he only drinks beer now. But it's a constant thing, just enough to keep him numb. He doesn't talk to me at all. And, uh, I've held a lot of hostility and anger, and I'm sure still do, toward him for that, and in fact only up until about three or four weeks ago, was I able to actually forgive each of my parents—not forgive exactly, but to let the past be past, and understand each of them as human beings, and know that they have their problems, and decide that what I needed to do was to give them love and try to bring some happiness for each of them into their life, if I can do that.

Dr. Miller: So where do you hold your anger toward your dad? Where is it in your body?

Steve: In the center of my chest. But—I don't feel that anger now as much as I have. I admit that I'm sure it's still there. One doesn't work out something one has spent thirty-eight years accumulating in a few days. I just don't believe it happens that way.

Dr. Miller: Right.

Steve: But I've begun the process of trying to love this man. Because he desperately needs the love. He's alone. He has his bottle of beer, and that's it. I had my cocaine. And I understand that now. So....

Dr. Miller: Laura told me you were feeling suicidal last night. Is that accurate?

Steve: Yes, that's accurate. If I'd'a left here, I'd've committed suicide.

Dr. Miller: You'd've what?

Steve: I would have committed suicide if I'd'a left here. Either through drugs or some other means. That's how far out I was. I've been like this many, many times during my life. Because I was denying myself.

Dr. Miller: Who are the three people in the world that you have the most anger toward? In your anger bag?

Steve: Uh, number one, there's myself. Number two is my mother, and number three is my father.

Dr. Miller: Put yourself on the chair.

Steve: You want me to sit there?

Dr. Miller: No, no. Make believe this is the you that you're angry at.

Steve: Okay....

Dr. Miller: And I'd like you to express some of that anger toward yourself.

Steve: Well, I honestly don't feel that anger right now. I have a lot of love for myself.

Dr. Miller: So the anger from last night is gone?

Steve: I feel some residuals from it, but a great deal of it is gone, yeah.

Dr. Miller: I make the assumption that suicide is anger turned inward.

Steve: Yes, it is.

Dr. Miller: You agree.

Steve: Absolutely.

Dr. Miller: So that's what I'm trying to get at with you now.

Steve: Right, I understand.

Dr. Miller: The residual, the anger...that energy that you were turning inward to make you want to kill yourself.

Steve: I don't feel like hitting me. I think the man's beautiful.

Dr. Miller: Okay. Do we have another method we might use to help you release some of the anger that you were turning in on yourself to feel suicidal? A punching bag under the tree? Would you be able to get into that? I want some physical means of expression for you....

Steve: I understand. I'm trying to, trying to get that out. I don't feel that.

Dr. Miller: Okay.

Steve: I feel that, uh, I don't feel that I need to beat up. I feel that I need to be loved. I feel that I need to give my love, which I don't think I've done, exactly. I think I've always done it with restriction. With expectation. And, uh, I think that's, I think that this man needs love.

Dr. Miller: What about this man who's sitting with the anger in his chest?

Steve: I don't know. I don't know. I, I feel that. But I don't feel like beating up on this guy.

Dr. Miller: Can you make the sound of that anger?

Steve: I'm not sure I could make the sound. But I can, I can tell you it's a very, very lonely cry. I don't know what that cry is, but, uh, it's pretty horrid....

Dr. Miller: The sound of that crying?

Steve: Oh yes.

Dr. Miller: Will you make the sound?

Steve: Uh, it would be a terrifically loud and awe...awing sound. You would like me to do that?

Dr. Miller: Please.

[Long pause.]

Steve: [Short loud scream.] [Pause.] That was real close.

Dr. Miller: Go for one more?

Steve: Yeah. [Pause.] [Slightly longer scream.]

Dr. Miller: Closer.

Steve: Yeah. Not through yet, am I?

Dr. Miller: No.

Steve: [Long pause.] I don't feel the need to do it any...I just....

Dr. Miller: Okay.

Steve: Yeah, that's total absolute aloneness, and uh, insanity. That's how I felt. I had told Dr. Miller a couple of days ago that, up until ninety days ago, I always thought that I was insane. Always. And I continue having doubts. And I have begun a process, I had begun a process, and I'm finding out more about it, and I've learned many, many tools here. And one of the biggest things I learned was today. About denying myself. I was always told to be normal. Well, there is no normal. but I was always told to be normal. Well, when you're so unnormal as I am, that's real tough. And so I've always tried to identify, connect myself from a lower plane, a lower cultural bullshit petty plane, and I could never do it. That's not me. I didn't know anyone else, nor ever have any other communication with anyone else that would lead me to believe that I was real. So I was unreal.

Dr. Miller: And now?

Steve: And right now I feel some anxiety, and I'm curious about it.

Dr. Miller: Are you real?

Steve: I'm becoming real. I've always been unreal. I'm becoming real. I can see realness. I can see beauty.

Dr. Miller: Are you in touch with the people in this room? Are you in touch with me right now?

Steve: I'm in touch with you.

Dr. Miller: Yes.

Steve: I'm in touch with some of the people in this room.

Dr. Miller: I'm going to make a sound now, you mimic the sound I make, okay?

Steve: Okay.

Dr. Miller: Rrrrrrowhrrrrr!

Steve: Rrrowhrrr!

Dr. Miller: Make your sound to the same amplitude that I make mine.

Steve: Okay.

Dr. Miller: Rrrrrrowhrrrrr!!!

Steve: Rrrowhrrr!

Dr. Miller: Come on, you've got a big chest.

Steve: Mine's not as loud as yours. Well....

Dr. Miller: [To Mike.] You point to, you give him a signal, all right, you give him a signal if his needs to be louder, alright?

Mike: Oh, I love it.

Dr. Miller: Rrrrrrowhrrrrr!!!

Steve: Rrrowhrrr!

Mike: [To Dr. Miller.] Yours is louder.

Dr. Miller: Just go like this to him, to bring his up. Okay, you do another one now.

Steve: Rrrowhrrr!

Dr. Miller: That's right, give him the signal.

Steve: You're kidding.

Mike: No.

Dr. Miller: Want to pick a different ref?

Steve: That's interesting. Rrrowhrrr!! Rrrrowhrrrr!! Rrrrrowhrrrr!! Sorry, can't roll the r.

Dr. Miller: Just bring up the volume.

Steve: You're kidding.

Dr. Miller: No.

Steve: I said that. Yeah. Rrrrrowhrrrr!! Now, that had to be louder than his.

Mike That was....

Steve: Rrrrrowhrrrr!! Rrrrrowhrrrr!!

Dr. Miller: Open up your throat. Otherwise you'll catch here.

Steve: Okay. Rrrrraaaahhh!

Dr. Miller: Well...?

Mike: Tie.

Dr. Miller: Pretty close okay, good. Rrrrraaaahhh!!!!

Steve: Rrrrraaaahhh!

Mike: Sorry.

Steve: You're kidding. That's, that's incredible.

Mike: Do you trust me or not?

Steve: Yes! Rrrrraaaahhh!! Weak, huh?

Mike: You're holding back.

Steve: Yes. Okay. [Bites his lip.]

Dr. Miller: Give me a roar this time.

Steve: Rrrrrowhrrrr!!

Dr. Miller: Rrrrrrowhrrrrr!!!

Steve: Rrrrrowhrrrr!!!

Dr. Miller: Feel the difference?

Steve: Yes.

Dr. Miller: Okay, bring one up now real low, this way. Rrrrrowhrrrrr!!!

Steve: Rrrrrowhrrrr!!!

Dr. Miller: All right!

Steve: Yeah! Scared *me*. [Bites his lip.]

Dr. Miller: Practice those. Your work is perfect for it, you're out in the hills, you can practice. Okay?

Mike: Just don't start an avalanche!

Dr. Miller: You've been doing this to yourself. [Gestures the biting of fingers.]

Steve: No kidding.

Dr. Miller: Mmm....You've been biting yourself.

Steve: Hmmm....

Dr. Miller: I see you biting yourself, so do an exercise as if you're biting somebody else. Turn the energy outward instead of inward.

Steve: Makes sense, yes.

Dr. Miller: Instead of fighting yourself like that...make the...roar.

Steve: Uh-huh, I'm just totally not aware....

Dr. Miller: Yes, I know that...make the roar. Get the self-biting out. Because that's part of that self-depression. That energy going in again. And you need exercises to get that energy flowing out of you rather than in. That's the reason that jogging and exercise work so well for depression. Because depression is de-pression, it's turning in energy on ourselves, with these mind games, the catastrophic expectations I talked about, making ourselves feel bad, the self-mutilation games we've seen us play during the week…energy turning in. And physical exercise is a way of turning the flowing outside of you rather than roaring at yourself inside, in your head.

Steve: Right. I also made a connection with the exercise, the stretching this morning. And that was throwing myself into the exercise, whatever the direction of it, throwing myself into it. The leglifts—painful, but I threw myself into that. Into, threw energy, took my energy and threw it into my foot.

Dr. Miller: Mmm-hmm.

Steve: And I also was able to relax at the same time. And it was a very rewarding experience.

Mike: Steve?

Steve: Sir?

Mike: I just wanna check on something. Did you, before you were talking about the exercise, did you understand what Dr. Miller was saying about the feel—about expressing your feelings outward instead of inward?

Steve: Let's assume I don't.

Mike: I just thought there was a lack of an acknowledgment.

Steve: There's something I have against screaming. Yes. I once tried screaming under water, I didn't do it. [Hunches over and bites his lip.]

Dr. Miller: Stop right there! There's the bite. Stay right in that position.

Steve: You're right!

Dr. Miller: You feel it?

Steve: Hey!

Dr. Miller: Now make a roar.

Steve: Rrrrrowhrrrr!!! Hey, good. I'll work on that.

Dr. Miller: Okay.

Steve: Yeah! Huh.

Dr. Miller: Okay, you want to get in touch with the bite, and instead of chewing yourself out, chew out somebody else. In fantasy, it doesn't have to be in reality.

Steve: Uh-huh.

Dr. Miller: This is a real good example of do unto others as you are doing to yourself.

Steve: [Laughs.] Okay.

MEETING THE ADDICT

Meeting the addict must be the work not only of the addiction-treating therapist, but also of the patients being treated for addiction. Here, Dr.

Miller asks key questions of a new group member, Jack, questions that quickly reveal the current life style and the treatment goals of the newcomer's addiction. Group members learn about themselves and their peers by listening to these exchanges. Eventually, they participate in the process, taking over portions of it from the therapist.

Dr. Miller: We have a new partner with us this evening. Some of you have already met Jack. I told you he was coming from parts southwest. One of the things we did last night, Jack, is that everybody went around and we introduced ourselves, and I did some interviewing of people, with particular reference to drug use. And everybody did that, the staff, as well as the participants, the partners in the program. So if you'd be so kind as to introduce yourself, tell us something about you, with particular reference to what you're doing here, and what your involvement in the world of drugs and alcohol is.

Jack: I mostly freebase. Cocaine.

Dr. Miller: How much base do you do? What's your average weekly consumption?

Jack: Four or five grams a day, something like that.

Dr. Miller: Uh-huh. What's your goal with regard to this program?

Jack: I don't know. Moderation, or elimination. Moderation would be my first goal. If I can't do that, I'm going to have to stop altogether. I'm not happy with the prospect of stopping, a life without coke. I prefer moderation.

Dr. Miller: You like the stuff a lot, huh? You love it. Tell me a couple of things you love about it.

Jack: The nice little high....

Dr. Miller: The high....

Jack: Right. And it's very....

Dr. Miller: An expensive mistress, isn't it?

Jack: The high is a very nice high.

Dr. Miller: Uh-huh. What time of day do you start basing?

Jack: It varies.

Dr. Miller: Varies. Varies, really? You base at work?

Jack: Outside of the office.

Dr. Miller: Now that you're a baser, do you snort any more?

Jack: Very rarely.

Dr. Miller: So it's not like you to carry some snort around with you? Since you don't base at the office, you could get a little snorting in.

Jack: Yeah. Some. I like the high.

Dr. Miller: You like the high, I heard that.

Jack: Other than that, I don't know that there are that many things to like about it.

Dr. Miller: Well, does it make you more social? Are you social with the base pipe, or do you tend to be alone?

Jack: Well, I'm social with the person or people I'm basing with, no one else.

Dr. Miller: Do you have a basing crowd? Basing buddies?

Jack: Most everybody I know bases, everybody I know is involved in some way with cocaine. Using it or dealing it. I guess my social life *is* cocaine.

Dr. Miller: What kind of effect does it have on your dating life? Any?

Jack: There is general cocaine consumed during the date, because I only date, or usually date....

Dr. Miller: Go on.

Jack: Only date someone who bases.

SEEING FAMILY AND PERSONAL RELATIONSHIPS

The open examination of perceptions of and feelings about family and personal relationships can become an important part of group therapy experience. Because of the tremendous role of co-addicts and codependents in the addiction and recovery process, such examination is not only important, but is a must in addiction-focused psychotherapy. The spouse and/or the entire family may come in for family therapy and may also join in for some or all of group therapy. When this does not occur, the therapist must nevertheless be certain that family relationships are addressed in group therapy. Group therapy participants benefit greatly by studying other members' relationship patterns.

Susan: Not everybody...

Dr. Miller: Tell 'em.

Susan: Well, for those of you who have not heard, I called my house right after dinner, and my twelve-year-old answered, and I said, "Angie, I don't want to ask to speak to Christine, so just don't say anything." She said, "Oh, Mom, you don't have to worry about anything. Christine's not here." I said, "Well, can I speak to David?" and she said, "Oh, he's at the dealer's house." I said, "Oh, God!" She said, "Oh, no, you have it all wrong, Mom. He packed up all of Christine's things, told her that if she didn't get in the car he was going to call the police and have her removed bodily. He has driven her over to the dealer's house and is going to see to it that she does not return to the house."

[Applause from group.]

And she says, "And one more surprise, Mom." She says, "You know David and his weed? His most treasured possession? He just gave it all away to his good friend Joe." David's been smoking weed since he was twelve.

Mark: Why'd he do that? For your sake?

Susan: Mmm-hmm. He said that when I return, there would be no drugs in the house....

Jack: Terrific. Hey, wow, that's super.

Susan: ...that I was more important than his use of cocaine or weed or anything else. That, as far as Christine was concerned, he knew that I was far more important than she was. I mean, this is coming out of my twelve-year-old's mouth, and I was real, real pleased. And she says, "Are you havin' a good time?" and I said, "Well, it's a lot of hard work and a lot of tears," and I said, "But yes, I'm having a wonderful time because I'm gettin clean. I'm getting straight." And she says, "Oh, we're going to be like the other families in the neighborhood!"

Jack: Terrific. That's terrific. I see you've got eye shadow on. That must mean you're feelin' better.

[Laughter.]

Susan: No, I don't have eye shadow on. But thank you. Maybe that's just dark circles.

Jack: No, up there....

Mark: Those aren't dark circles!

Jack: Sounds like David's a helluva man.

Susan: He's much more of a man than I am a woman, puttin' it mildly. He's an amazing young man, because he's given so much time to my care for the last three years. And it goes to show you that good foundations can really do things for the young people.

Dr. Miller: Now say some nice things about yourself and what you've done for him.

Susan: Well, I made him into a drug addict! No, I take that back. I...I don't take on that responsibility. I may have paid for it, but I, because he is as smart as he is, he had the free choice. I won't take...I used to take on the responsibility of different people's drug problems, but I realize that I can't take on responsibility for the whole world, just what I did to myself. But anyway, I'm pleased with me...I'm making progress. That's about all the good I can say about myself. I tend to slice myself in little pieces.

Jack: What did you do for David?

Susan: What I did for David? Um...I gave him a home when his father threw him out. And I guess I taught him, and he taught me, what real genuine friendship and love is about. Because this young man has really taught me what real embracing love of mankind is. See, we always think of love as between a male and a female, or a physical type love. But David's and my love is just, I'm number one, and he's number one also. And with him, he's number one, and I'm number one also. So. And this is a young man that's only nineteen himself. I once told him that his calling in life was to care and share with other people. He has dyslexia, which makes it very difficult to do a lot of work other than with his hands. But what he has in his heart to share with other people—and I see it with his friends and with me and with my twelve-year-old, and with other kids that are in the neighborhood, even though he was fucked up on drugs most of the time. He's fair. And he's taught me how to be real, real fair. And he's concerned. And he really cares for other people. But he also cares for himself, which is really amazing. See, I always thought that, if you put yourself number one that that was being real selfish. But he taught me that that's not. You know, that you have to look out for number one. And that's real hard for me to do. I always wonder what's going to happen to the next guy down the road, instead of what's gonna happen to me. Anyway, that's not the question you asked me! [Laughing.]

Jack: No, it wasn't.

Susan: I get on to these rambling things.

Jack: What have you done for David? You gave him a home when his father kicked him out....

Susan: Mmm-hmm.

Jack: And he found out what love was all about.

Susan: Yeah. That's a lot. And I've also provided well for him.

Jack: Sounds like you deserved what he did for you.

Susan: But he did that for me long before I ever did much for him, though. You know, one time I said, "If you don't get your act together, I'm gonna throw you out." And he said, "No, you're not. Because I'm not goin' anywhere. Because you need me." He said, "You need me to give you the support you need until you kick your drugs." And he said, "So, if you want me out of this house, you'll just have to call the police. Because until I know you're okay, I'm not leaving." And that was his comeback to me. Which, you know, made me feel really good. Gave me hope.

"I am an addict and you will kill me."

6

Leaving Chemical Dependence Behind: The Longest Goodbye

Let thine intent
Be not misconstruing
Let not thy will
To cause confusion.
As the one power
Provides the answer to the question
Of the origin of creative genius,
So it is death
That ripens the rose.

(Contributed by an Anonymous Group Therapy Participant)

This is the third of three chapters written around transcripts of Dr. Miller's group therapy sessions. Included in this chapter are some of the closing discussions and activities of the week-long residential intensive component of his Cokenders Alcohol and Drug Program. One of these activities is the desensitization exercise, which Dr. Miller often repeated several times for its cumulative effect. This exercise provides patients an opportunity to say "no" to an offer of drugs and alcohol. Repeated offers or "challenges" help patients to "reprogram" themselves, to acquire new responses, such as "No thanks, I'm an addict." Because of its great value in addiction-focused psychotherapy, I will detail the exercise here.

DESENSITIZATION PSYCHOTHERAPY

Neutralizing the conditioned response, the response that includes using drugs and alcohol, is basic to recovery from addiction. In the famous experiment by Ivan Pavlov, a hungry dog is presented with a piece of meat. The dog salivates. This stimulus *is repeated several times. The meat is called the* unconditioned stimulus, *and the salivation is called the* unconditioned response. *In step two, every time the meat is shown to the dog, a light bulb is turned on. Eventually, the light without the presence of meat will cause the dog to salivate. The light becomes the* conditioned stimulus, *and the salivation in the presence of the light is the* conditioned response.

Cocaine addiction has taught us a great deal about conditioned responses in chemical dependence. Cocaine is considered by many professionals to be the most reinforcing of all drugs. Part of their belief is based on an experiment in which laboratory monkeys, when given a choice of cocaine or food or sex, repeatedly chose cocaine until they died of starvation. In the case of humans, the feeling of pleasure or elation is often so great that they too will eventually choose cocaine over food or sex. After a certain number of experiences with the drug, a person will also begin to have a reaction to even the mention of the drug: The mention of the drug elicits a conditioned response. Conditioned responses to the presence and even the thought of the cocaine include: sweaty palms, increased heart rate, facial flush, tingling in the lungs, and an increase in the general level of arousal. Addicted people feel such conditioned responses and then attempt, sometimes at great cost in money, energy, and reputation, to get the drug or drugs to which they are addicted into their bodies by their preferred method of ingestion.

In order to neutralize the conditioned response, the following exercise was designed. Group members are told to remain silent during the exercise, until the end when they will be asked to speak. They are instructed to pay close attention to their responses and then to write down any and all physical, emotional, and mental reactions they have during the exercise. These patients have been given precise lessons in becoming highly aware of such internal reactions in previous sessions.

Group members are seated on armchairs that have been arranged in a circle around a circular table. Each of them is about 8 feet from the *closest edge of the table. Dr. Miller opens a large box and very slowly places the contents on the circular table. The contents of the box includes an extremely wide variety of the paraphernalia used by addicted persons: prescription and over-the-counter pills; bottles of alcohol, beer, and wine; marijuana papers and rolling machines; cocaine bottles, bindles, spoons, straws, razor blades, grinders, scales, rolled up $100 bills, mirrors, base pipes, screens, torches, baking soda, ether, plastic tubing, hypodermic needles, cotton, and 20-gram mounds of what looks like pure cocaine; plastic bags containing what looks like heroin and "speed" or methedrine; and many other drugs and paraphernalia. During one of these exercises, a woman who could no longer control herself began to cry and exclaimed, "Oh my God, that table is my entire life for the last three years."*

After all the materials are on the table, the group members are asked to write and then to read aloud their lists of physical and emotional reactions to the stimuli on the table. They are encouraged to use various tools such as abdominal breathing, self-massage, and progressive relaxation to neutralize their conditioned responses. With practice, they can eventually sit in the room and experience little or no response to the stimuli on the table. These once-overpowering stimuli will appear as what they really are when stripped of their perceived power: old glass, dirty plastic, scratched metal, various bits of paper, liquids of all types, white and other colored powders, pills, and other powerless materials.

During the reprogramming phase, the group members are taught how to say "no" when presented with the stimuli. Each participant is offered his or her drugs of choice and related paraphernalia and told to give one of these responses:

1. *No thanks, I've quit.*
2. *I'd love some, and I won't.*
3. *I'm an addict, and you'll kill me.*
4. *Another way of strongly saying no.*

During the reprogramming phase of this exercise, participants practice using these responses and adding other personalized responses to their repertoires. The combination of neutralizing the conditioned internal response and reprogramming the verbal response increases the possibility of saying "no" in the similar but real-life situations most group members will find in the near and distant future.

One of the most fascinating and intense scenes in Dr. Miller's addiction-focused therapy is his use of the above-described exercise to do desensitization psychotherapy. As detailed above, this involves presenting patients with an array of objects of their addictions. Recall that the patients are asked, first, to record their reactions on paper, and then to share and work on their reactions with the group. These reactions are prime material for group work. I have condensed one of these sessions in the transcript below.

Dr. Miller: I put the cocaine out first.

Joan: Really?

Dr. Miller: The coke was out before the booze. Did you find yourself more interested in the booze than the coke?

Joan: In both. But I was surprised how much I wanted the booze. I'm a coke addict, not a drinker....

Dr. Miller: Okay. Now the next thing is to start building up habit patterns of saying "no." It's a habit. Saying no, saying yes. They're simply habits. You can make new habits. So I'm going to go around the circle. I'm going to offer you your drugs of choice and I want you to say either, "No, thanks, I've quit," "I'd *love* some, and I won't," "I'm an addict, and you'll kill me," or some other reply that means "no," one that you yourself have designed. It's "No, thanks, I've quit," "I'd *love* some, and I won't," "I'm an addict, and you'll kill me," or some other form of "no" that you can use over and over again any time somebody puts a base pipe or some coke or some alcohol or some pot or some other drug in front of you. Anytime this happens, out will come that "no." Because one of the *hows* of how to maintain your resolve is to have tools, is to be prepared, is to have contingencies. Because we all know that once you take that first drink or that first snort or that first hit, you're likely to go on using the whole evening. And then you'll be through this thing of, "Well, I'll start quitting again tomorrow." There's no such thing, after quitting drugs, like deciding that you're going to take just one little bit, just to see what it's like. Not when there's a pile of it in front of you. The only way you're gonna take one little line is if you're on an island, and there's only one line on the island. Okay, you know what the responses are?

So, for the next exercise, folks, I'd like you to settle yourselves in your chairs, take out your notebooks....They will be necessary. Joan, do you have something that you can write on?

Susan: Janet and I are gonna be standing a lot, because her back hurts and I can't stay awake, so we're gonna kind of reinforce each other. So if you see us both hopping up, you'll know that that's what, that she's helping me stay awake, and it's gonna help her back.

Dr. Miller: Okay. What I'd like you to do is get your notebooks in front of you, and your pens....

[Noises of people rustling paper, etc.]

It's important for the next exercise that you maintain total silence from the time we start until I ask you to speak. And what I want you to do during this exercise is write down any physical or psychological or mental responses that you have: Anything you notice about your body, any kind of things that go on in your mind. If you see other people doing things, fidgeting, or anything else, you might make a note of that. What I don't want you to do is to talk, or to get out of your chairs. All right? So it'll be completely silent except for the note writing, until such time as I ask you to speak, and then I will be asking you to talk about the things that you've written down. If you have questions, now's the time.

Mike: The feelings and emotions inside of us right now? The things that we're feeling or doing: What should we write?

Dr. Miller: I'm going to be presenting things, objects, drugs and so on, to you, and you'll be responding or not responding to these things. Okay? And if you have a response, I want you to write it down. If you have a feeling in your body, I want you to write it down. If you have a thought in your mind, I want you to write it down. Or if you see somebody else do something that stands out for you, write it down. But mostly I'm interested in your own *inner* responses—the ones in your own body and your own mind. Okay?...So from here on until I start the discussion, we'll be silent. Thank you.

[Long silence, sounds of Dr Miller chopping what appears to be cocaine, preparing drugs and drinks, and dumping out paraphernalia, alcohol, cigarettes, candy, cookies, etc. After the long silence, Dr. Miller asks the group to check in.]

Dr. Miller: So. Let's begin.

Joan: Immediately, my mouth started to salivate when I saw the, uh, whiskey. And I started to sniff when I saw what was supposed to be cocaine (whether or not it really is). Then, when I saw the cigarettes, I didn't notice anything. But then I saw the carton of cigarettes, I wished there were more of them. Then, when I saw the olives, I wanted to have a martini. Then the Reese's Pieces and the cookies, I thought, "I'd prefer something else with my drink." The paraphernalia doesn't do anything to me. The pills didn't do anything either. And I thought, I can't see them too well, I thought those there were champagne glasses.

Dr. Miller: And what about other parts of your inner experience, the sensations in your body?

Joan: Well, I had a longing for a drink. My mouth was salivating, and I started to sniff when I saw the cocaine.

Dr. Miller: Anything else? Notice any movement in your body?

Joan: I saw myself moving.

Dr. Miller: Mmmmm? You saw yourself moving towards the table? The bourbon?

Joan: Just to see what it was. I think I recognize the brand. I can't see for sure, but I guess that's champagne over there, and that's vodka, that's gin. But you know what? It didn't matter that much. I really didn't want the stuff. I was just reacting to it.

Dr. Miller: Which of these bottles would you like to drink out of? You, sir? A little base?

Mike: Uh...

Dr. Miller: Anything missing here? I got some, uh, baking soda, a little ether, what do you need?

Mike: Mmm...not a thing, thank you.

Dr. Miller: ...full pipe?

Mike: No. I'd like to, but I won't.

Dr. Miller: Susan? A little coke? A little pick-me-up? You won't be so tired in this room....

Susan: I'll handle my tiredness on my own. I don't need that.

Dr. Miller: Leslie?

Leslie: [Clears throat and hesitates.] I'm an addict, and you'll kill me.

Dr. Miller: You're right. [Pause.] Thomas?

Thomas: No. I'll die if I do.

Dr. Miller: You sure?

Thomas: Yes.

Dr. Miller: You drink a little? How 'bout starting a little, take a little drink instead of your other drugs, take care of you in the snow...it's cold up there. Can I get you something to drink?

Thomas: No, no thanks.

Dr. Miller: Little toot? Got some nice rocks here....

Phil: They look good, yes, but uh...I'd love some, but no thanks, I'm driving.

Janet: [Laughing.] That's what he always says. Give him a graham cracker, he says, "No thanks, I'm driving." "No thanks, it's against my religion."

Dr. Miller: Come on! Nobody's gonna believe a story like that. Look at these nice rocks!

Janet: I always, I always....

Dr. Miller: Look at these nice rocks I've got here and here. I'm sure we could turn this over and get some of that....

Janet: Oh, I'm sure we could.

Dr. Miller: How 'bout it?

Janet: That's all right.

Dr. Miller: Little bit?

Janet: The more you egg me on, the more "no" I'm gonna say, so you might as well not ask me. [Pause.] I always used to always say everything was against my religion.

Dr. Miller: Okay.

Mike: Janet, you're really not interested in this stuff?

Janet: Aren't you going back to him? Not right now. Now right now. While he was putting it out I was very amazed, like this. And I doubted if it was real, so that gives me some wonder about myself, 'cause why the fuck would I care if it's real or not if I wasn't gonna do it?

Dr. Miller: Exactly!

Janet: So I know that.

Dr. Miller: Good for you. That's a good observation.

Janet: And I didn't know...I was expecting some questions for some reason. But...I feel better now than I did when you were pullin' it out.

Dr. Miller: Okay. Okay, what I'd like you all to do now is to get up and, in silence, go down for lunch. You can talk while you're eating, but just in the few steps from here until you get your lunch plate, I'd just like some of this to sink in. Give yourself a chance to think about your response, about what your response was to this, and about making new responses that are going to give you the freedom to say "no." I will see you all this evening.

[The group later reconvenes for an evening session]

Dr. Miller: Take out your books, and once again, take a look at the materials...note any reaction that you're having, or any thoughts, little comments to yourself....

[Long silence, except for paper rustling, people shifting in their seats, and other background noises.]

Dr. Miller: Remember that one fellow handed in his paraphernalia here, and then he came back a month later and he wanted to know where it was. He didn't see it in the pile. And then, finally he saw it, it was under there, it was a special, a bullet, it was that bullet thing, remember? [One or two group members nod.] Couldn't find it, wanted to know where his bullet was, he thought somebody took it.

Mike: That there gold thing?

Janet: I can spot a bullet a mile away.

Dr. Miller: Right.

Mike: What's that?

Mark: What's a bull?

Janet: A bull-it, upside down, you keep it in your purse or in your pocket and you go [she sniffs]. [There is laughter among the group.] They always break, too....

Dr. Miller: Isn't it nice, now you don't have to care at all about....

Mike: It's amazing some of the things we come up with, ways to use and keep our stuff, isn't it?

Dr. Miller: Did you bring in the book, the paraphernalia catalogue? I wanted to read something from the book. Mike, did you read that section where it lists the various coke-using things you can buy?

Mike: I couldn't even get past the front page!

Janet: Yeah, you can buy a bullet for $120.

Dr. Miller: For $120? Huh? Did you read that? There's a copy around here somewhere. You know where it is, will you get it? Okay, what reactions did you have tonight, if any, to this assortment?

Joan: Well, actually, I was a little disappointed at first, because at first, I had no reactions at all. And then I went, "Oops, I just changed." I noticed a little bit of salivating but I don't know exactly what I was salivating for. I can't pinpoint it but, uh, I don't know if it's 'cause I'm very full from dinner. Uh...all this stuff certainly made much less of an impact this time, this evening, than it did this afternoon....

Dr. Miller: How about you, Peggy? Any reaction? Nothing this time. Dick, nothing happening?

Dick: No. Not at all.

Dr. Miller: Allan, these bullets? Did you have any physical reaction to them?

Allan: Just a headache.

Dr. Miller: You got the headache, just as soon as you saw the bullets? Or did you have it before?

Allan: I think I had it before, but I felt it much stronger when I saw the stuff.

Dr. Miller: Susan?

Susan: I almost started hyperventilating!

Dr. Miller: I hear you had a tremendous amount of energy downstairs.

Susan: Yeah. [Laughing.] Like a tornado! [Laughter.] Speed without speed. Interesting.

Dr. Miller: Somebody told me the way to have her have a lot of energy in group is to get her to do some cleaning and scrubbing! [Laughter.]

Susan: And I'm a terrible housekeeper, that's what's so funny. Tonight I washed most of the dishes myself.

Dr. Miller: You used to be a terrible housekeeper.

Susan: Yeah. Well, I used to not be, and then I became a lousy housekeeper, and now I'm gonna be a lousy housekeeper. That stuff really bothers me, it really does.

Dr. Miller: What stuff is that?

Susan: All that! [Pointing at the table full of paraphernalia.]

Dr. Miller: What?

Susan: All that.

Dr. Miller: What?

Susan: The paraphernalia.

Dr. Miller: The paraphernalia?

Susan: I don't like it being around. It bothers me.

Dr. Miller: Where? Where does it bother you?

Susan: In my stomach.

Dr. Miller: What is the sensation in your stomach?

Susan: I most probably could have told you five minutes ago, but I tuned out again. There's something I'm not dealing with, because I keep tuning it out, you know. It's like I'm already out. Just turn me off and on. As soon as I walked in I looked down at it all. It was like instant nausea. And then I sat down and I started to breathe, and I couldn't, and then Peggy said, "Just like this," and she knew I was trying and I couldn't. And then I almost started crying again…and then, it's like—I just turned it off. And there was nothing.

Dr. Miller: You turned yourself off.

Susan: I mean, it was like an instant mechanism that I have. I don't like it being there, though. Even turned off, I don't like it being there.

Dr. Miller: Say it to that pile of stuff. Say, "I don't like your being there."

Susan: I don't like you being there.

Dr. Miller: Say it again.

Susan: I don't like you being here [starting to cry].

Dr. Miller: One more time, Susan.

Susan: I don't like you being here.

Dr. Miller: Now tell that pile of stuff what's going on inside of you, because it's there.

Susan: I don't, I don't, I don't *know*. I *don't* know what's going on inside of me. I just know that I don't like it being here.

Dr. Miller: Again.

Susan: I don't like you being here.

Dr. Miller: Breathe.

Susan: I have another *why* question, but I won't ask it.

Dr. Miller: Sure, ask it first, and then we'll listen and we'll learn from your *why* question.

Susan: Why is it not bothering everybody else like it's bothering me?

Dr. Miller: Okay, now I'll translate the question.

Susan: Okay.

Dr. Miller: "There must be something wrong with me since I'm having a reaction and other people aren't. I must be sick, bad, crazy, or stupid."

Susan: Okay.

Dr. Miller: Got it?

Susan: Got it. That still doesn't….

Dr. Miller: It doesn't answer the accusation.

Susan: I know.

Dr. Miller: Because you can never answer an accusation. All you can do is make a comment to yourself, "Ah! There I go again. I'm accusing myself. And how am I doing it? I'm comparing my feelings to other people's feelings. There must be something wrong with me, if I'm feeling so strongly right now, and nobody else is. I must be sick, bad, crazy, and stupid."

Susan: What if *they're* sick, bad, crazy, or stupid?

Dr. Miller: That's right. Or neither one of you are. You're having your feelings, they're having their feelings. We don't all feel at the same time. So you're using a means of comparison now.

Susan: I can just imagine what would happen if I went home to all that, and I had almost equally as much paraphernalia, I had so much paraphernalia it took about six boxes to hold it.

Dr. Miller: Where is it now?

Susan: It's—it's all gone now.

Dr. Miller: Is it? Too bad, I'd like to have it for these archives.

Susan: Except for three bongs, which David cannot find; Christine has hidden them. He says they're somewhere in the house, and he says he's looked everywhere, but....You know, I...I can look, I could look at my stuff at home and it didn't...there was no reaction, like this...I didn't let myself notice my reactions at home, I guess.

Dr. Miller: Of course!

Susan: The alcohol, see, doesn't bother me, or the pills, that doesn't bother me. It's just all that other....

Dr. Miller: How 'bout this nice neat tray, out here?

Susan: The lines layin' there, they—they don't bother me, um....The bong does. I have no desire to use that. That's not what the problem is. I don't know if it's disgust or anger or...I just don't know what I'm feeling, but I can tell you one thing, I'm feeling something!

Dr. Miller: Mmm-hmmm. Mmm-hmm....Will you make the sound of your feeling? Can you do that?....No, not right now....That's okay. Well, let's go along, and find out what other people....

Susan: I know what I'm feeling! I'm feeling sadness.

Dr. Miller: Ah!

Susan: [Crying.] That's what it is. It's sadness. 'Cause, you see, I never looked at my paraphernalia like I'm looking at this paraphernalia. It sums up three and a half years of my life for me. That's what.

Dr. Miller: Mmm-hmm.

Susan: And that's sad.

Dr. Miller: That's three and a half years of your life.

Susan: Yeah. [Crying louder.] Three and a half very valuable years. Gone. Wasted.

Dr. Miller: Mmm-hmm. Every year is valuable.

Susan: Why don't we just buy that much fake money and throw a couple of hundred thousand dollars up on top of that stuff. Money is part of it all.

[Dr. Miller stands up, leaves the circle, and returns with money, large and small bills, which he sprinkles over the pile of drugs and paraphernalia.]

Dr. Miller: Well, perhaps some of your tears are saying good-bye to an old friend. You ready to say goodbye?

Susan: I'm just sad that I had to wait—that it took so long to say good-bye.

Dr. Miller: Some people believe that the more you love something, the longer it take to grieve its loss. People who do a lot of family therapy and marital therapy tell me that half the time the love lasted is how long it takes you to grieve the loss of that love. So if you were basing cocaine for three and a half years, it may take you a year and three-quarters. I certainly suggest that everybody in this room who's been connected to coke and booze and whatever else, give strong consideration to putting as much time and energy into putting this thing behind you, as you did into putting this thing into you. 'Cause you're not going to build up a habit over a period of weeks, months, years, thirteen years, or whatever...and just all of a sudden wave it goodbye, as if it never existed. You've got to be prepared to do the work, the ongoing work. And you've got to be prepared for these contingencies that we've been talking about, for this thing to come back, to come back at you.... You've got to be prepared to live day to day, and to be looking around in this whole world for what you can find that'll nourish your existence, that'll make your soul feel good. Something instead of booze and other drugs. 'Cause obviously, if drugs had been doing the trick, you wouldn't be here. So drugs don't do the trick.

Susan: You know, I look at at that, and I think, "How...?" [Mumbles.]

Dr. Miller: Once again, please?

Susan: I look at all that, and all I can say to myself is, "How could I have allowed that to totally control me for three and a half years?" What are we looking for? What was I looking for? You know? I sure as hell never found it!

Dr. Miller: You can express your appreciation before you say good-bye. Like you might do to a lover. For the things that you appreciate. What did you get that you loved?

Susan: I really don't know. I had to have gotten something, otherwise I couldn't....See, when I look at it, all I can see is three and a half years and all this money. And a confused head, and a broken heart. And I don't know why. And I don't know how it happened. Or why it happened.

Dr. Miller: Today's the first day of the rest of your life.

Susan: Out of everything that's happened to me since I've been here, this, this is the—this tops it. Everything. I have never felt so much in my whole life as I have felt twice today looking at this pile of stuff. [Tears and sobbing.]

Dr. Miller: Bless your heart.

Susan: I mean...I know that I couldn't feel any worse over a death of my own child than to sit here and look at this.

Dr. Miller: This is what you need. You need to feel again. Because you've been cutting off most of your feelings for all these years.

Susan: I wanna....All of a sudden my sorrow has, like it's turned to anger, and it's, it's strange.

Dr. Miller: It's what?

Susan: I said, now I feel angry all of a sudden.

Dr. Miller: Uh-huh.

Susan: Like, "Damn you!" you know.

Dr. Miller: Let's hear it, Susan.

Susan: [Still crying, a little harder.] I can't.

Dr. Miller: Say, "I won't."

Susan: I won't.

Dr. Miller: Say, "I'll keep my anger to myself."

Susan: I'll keep my anger to myself. Now I understand what a psychiatrist once told me, that the line between hatred and love was so...was just a very thin one. And I guess she was right. 'Cause I hate it, I hate it, and yet, the other side of me loved it. And I don't love it anymore, but...I mean, three and a half years!

Dr. Miller: Again? Say it again?

Susan: Three and a half years!

Dr. Miller: Again?

Susan: Three and a half years!

Dr. Miller: Again?

Susan: Three and a half years!!

Dr. Miller: Again?

Susan: [Sobbing even more, and then yelling.] Three and a half years!!

Dr. Miller: ...Breathe! When was the last time you went ice skating?

Susan: Um, about three and a half years ago, I think, I don't, I can't even remember. I bought a new pair of skates and had a new pair of boots made, I think four years ago. And I wore them *one* time...I mean, it's difficult to skate and to base coke at the same time.

Dr. Miller: Well, that's one of the things that I will prescribe, then.

Susan: I'm going to go back to skating.

Dr. Miller: Skating? Several times a week?

Susan: Yeah. It's not very often that you go out and buy a pair of $300 skates and only put 'em on one time. They're a lot prettier than all that crap anyway.

Dr. Miller: Uh-huh. And last a lot longer than three grams, huh?

Susan: Sure will.

Dr. Miller: [Reading from a group member's notebook which was passed to him.] This says, "One gram of cocaine. What you get: a small paper packet or a vial filled with white powder. One gram. What else do you get for $120? Several hours of good food, drink and company? Two people can go to an excellent restaurant, to the movies and have a nightcap for $120. You can have a small party, spend about $10 a head on mineral water, enough to last a whole evening. You can get a nice pair of shoes for $60, new pants for $30, and a new shirt for $30. Or, you can buy a decent tape recorder for $120. Flowers, a bottle of perfume, and a surprise gift. Or a large bag full of new toys for the kids. You could be quite a hero for $120." I rather like this page. I think it's an interesting thing for everybody to think about. Think in terms of what your weekly expenditure on your addiction was, and what you can now do with the money.

Susan: I've said this to a few people, but I'd like to share it with the whole group. This is that, I guess it's what you call a real addiction. I have a beautiful twin-crew cabin cruiser that's paid for, that's mine. It has been in the water one time this year. It was in the water for about an hour and a half, because I was in a hurry to get back, so I could get back to my base pipe. I couldn't afford to take it out for a ride, because it held 300 gallons of gasoline; and yet, I could spend $1,000 a week on smoking cocaine. Try that one on for size. Ask me where my priorities are? So, anyway I figure for the price of a couple of grams of cocaine, I could take out eleven people on my boat and we could have a great party for a whole weekend without using drugs.

Dr. Miller: Have a helluva time on the bay, huh?

Susan: That's right. And the price is just a few grams of cocaine. I just wonder how I could get so involved in drugs, and not in clean fun.

Dr. Miller: The question now, Susan, is how to stay involved in the latter, and put the past behind.

Susan: One thing I have to be very careful of is that I have a real bad habit of chastising myself for ever and ever and ever and *ever*. So I have to work really hard at saying this is the past, it's over.

Dr. Miller: It's done. Now move on.

Susan: I have to close the book on it.

Dr. Miller: Yes.

Susan: That's the difficult part for me, because if I punish myself too much, I might go back to it.

Dr. Miller: That's correct. Absolutely correct.

Susan: And that's scary. I'm my own worst enemy. And I know that.

Dr. Miller: Mmm-hmm.

Susan: *Will* I forgive myself? [Goes into silence.]

Dr. Miller: Tom, any reaction from you this evening?

Thomas: Yeah. Yeah, I'd like to change the answer I gave you earlier. I believe you asked me a question, and I said, "No thank you, I've quit." I'd like to change that to, "Yeah, I would, but I won't."

Dr. Miller: Mmm-hmm. You want some. And you won't.

Thomas: That's correct.

Dr. Miller: Any physical reaction, as I, we, opened up the materials?

Thomas: No, I have much more of a reaction right now, after sitting here through all this, than I did when you started...but...I kept looking at those little innocent sleeping pills down there that I gave you. And realizing their connection to my other drugs. And also, I went through a period of time when I couldn't look at this stuff, it just, it drove me nuts. I couldn't look at it, I couldn't be around it, I was just absolutely in a dither, like she is, much the same. Couldn't look at it. Doesn't affect me that way now, it's been quite a while. But, uh, I couldn't be around it when I...about a week after I made this decision to quit. I could not handle seeing it talking about it—nothin'. Zero. But it got better. You get distance from it. Okay? Yeah, I'm okay, now, I think. Thanks, Richard.

Dr. Miller: You're welcome, Thomas....Leslie?

Leslie: The paraphernalia didn't bother me, but the money bothered me, but the money bothered me a lot...when you threw the money down. That's what really hit home. I want my money back [laugh], you know? All the, you know, thousands of dollars, hundreds of thousands of dollars I spent. I wasted it. I want it back. You know?

Mike: Hundreds of thousands of dollars?

Leslie: Six years of drugging and drinking.

Mike: Yeah, I guess.

Leslie: I never really added it up, but I'm sure it comes to at least a couple of hundred thousand. So that's what bothered me...the money.

Dr. Miller: Mmm-hmm. Something worth keepin' in mind, huh?

Leslie: Yeah. Money talks.

Dr. Miller: Money talks [Laughter.]

Mike: Susan was certainly right. It does....

Leslie: I thought, "Nice touch!" When you threw the money down, I looked at it and I thought, "Nice touch!" It really sort of topped it all off very nicely.

Dr. Miller: Yeah, we'll get a photo. I have a polaroid here, we'll get a photo of that.

Dr. Miller: Mmm-hmm. Phil?

Phil: Just an initial thought, when she talked about money. I wondered...you probably couldn't even see all that stuff with a million dollars over it, which I bet is a feasible figure.

Dr. Miller: For this room....

Phil: Yeah. One million dollars. One million dollars in $100 bills. That's a feasible figure, not totally out of range, I bet. Including money spent on habits and lifestyles connected to them.

Dr. Miller: Mmm-hmm.

Phil: That's hard to believe. But it's believable. Because we did it.

Dr. Miller: Yes.

Phil: I'm sorry, forget the *we*. *I* did it! Maybe half a million bucks.

Mike: How much total, what do you think you spent on coke?

Phil: That's a very difficult question to answer.

Dr. Miller: How much in money do you think you've used on cocaine in your lifetime?

Phil: I'd say a quarter-mil is a feasible figure. There again, you know, if you say a quarter million dollars, it's not just, you know, initially you don't do it alone, you know. If you do a gram, your friends do grams. You know? Initially, you don't do it alone, and you're a prince of a guy...[Laughter.] You know, tell me!

Susan: Good personality....

Dr. Miller: Good personality, right! I'll have to remember that one.

Phil: And the more I had, the more bubbly I was. Right, right! He didn't take a bath, doesn't matter, he's bubbly! I'd say a quarter of a million dollars is feasible. A quarter of a million goddamn dollars. I could have actually made it in the construction business with that! [Laugh.] I wouldn't have to be selling my house now. Uh, I don't know...I'm starting to feel uncomfortable, sitting here with all that stuff in front of me and thinking about other people smoking, basing.

Dr. Miller: Mmm-hmm. Where? Where are you feeling the discomfort? Remember, the first question, when you have a feeling....

Phil: And I can't make no sound, neither!

[Laughter.]

Dr. Miller: I'm not gonna ask you to make a sound.

Phil: I *can* make a sound of disgust, and hate, of anger, okay. But it's tough to feel, to make a sound of uncomfortableness and, uh, and confusion.

Dr. Miller: Okay. Instead, can you locate the discomfort?

Phil: Yeah. Seems to be, seems to be filling me up! I'm getting filled up with discomfort. I'm getting bloated, same way I used to get bloated when I used to do it. But now I'm getting boated by sitting here, uh, uh, in its presence. There again, like you say, you know, I was involved for three years. How do you become disinvolved in three days? Or four days, or five days?

Dr. Miller: Right.

Phil: So I would...I mean, even if I had a feeling or a craving for it, which I might, which I do, I, I would leave the room. Or I would not...I can't, I won't be around it, I won't bring it to work, which is what's gonna be the problem. And then I had other thoughts earlier. You know, uh, I based two or three times in my life. The more I talked about it....

Janet: The more you wanted it.

Phil: The more I heard about it...."It's unbelievable, it's the best, it's this, it's that..." I was thinking, "I know it is! Boy, I wouldn't mind doing some base!" And I don't base! And I don't care how good shooting up is, I don't want to shoot. But I actually gave thought to shooting; that's close enough. I actually just thought about it the last time I had done it, which was months and months and months ago, and I thought about how good shooting could be.

Janet: If it was that good, you would have continued doing it, wouldn't you?

Phil: Absolutely.

Janet: Well, then, it wouldn't have been that good. I mean, you based. If it was that good to you....

Phil: No, I didn't have the ...I didn't know how to do it, I didn't want to know how to do it. I had that much intelligence that I knew I couldn't do it. I knew that it would have been my total demise. It was my demise anyway, but shooting, even more than smoking it, basing, would have been my immediate demise.

Dr. Miller: And you're right.

Phil: I know I'm right.

Dr. Miller: You're absolutely right.

Phil: I know I'm right. I know I'm right. That would have been it—boom!

Dr. Miller: Look how fast you moved with your habit.

Phil: I knew I was doing that.

Janet: Now he's getting a craving for base just listening to us all talk about it, just being near the idea of it.

Phil: It has nothing to do with you, them, them, or them. It's a simple fact that it exists and I would've used it...it exists, period.

Dr. Miller: You know something? If the shooters were here, the shooters would be telling you how great it is to shoot....

Phil: Right.

Janet: He was saying, I don't think that he really had the urge until he heard us talk about it.

Dr. Miller: Anyway, it's academic....

Phil: The urge existed. This brought it out more so. But it had to be brought out anyways. I'm just trying to tell you how I felt.

Dr. Miller: That's right, and I'm glad we got that out.

Phil: Absolutely.

Janet: Okay.

Dr. Miller: And you? Any reaction at all?

Janet: I didn't have any until you told us to sit there and write. And then, uh, the first thing I saw is my graham crackers, and then I said, "Better diet; after all, you are what you eat." So I'm committed to a better diet. Uh....The lines look tempting, because I'm tired and I've got a backache right now, again. And that's what gets me going, you know, my pain and fatigue.

Dr. Miller: Uh-huh.

Janet: Uh, my, it's, I'm, I feel less tempted than I did this afternoon. When I saw you cut those lines and I, I looked at those, I wouldn't do it, but I, it looks good. Um. I feel like partying. It's the—I've got the end of the work week craving. You're gonna work Monday through Friday, and you're gonna expect a weekend. And what do we do usually? We booze and drug.

Mike: *I'm* gonna work Monday through Friday.

Joan: I'm gonna Monday through Friday, and then it's gonna, then the weekend's gonna come. And the way I used to celebrate the weekend (before I got *too* involved and drank and drugged all the time, back when I had a more moderate situation), was starting on Friday. I had what I thought was a moderate intake. It's the end of the week, I feel like partying. It reminds me of the time when I thought I could control it. Or that I could just do it on the weekend. And I think of the needle, which I've never even—I hate needles, I scream bloody murder whether the person's got it in me or hasn't even started yet, in the doctor's office, I'm the worst. [Laugh.] "Aaaaaah! It hurts!" when he hasn't even touched me with it yet. I picked up this needle on the table here, and all of a sudden I felt a lot of pressure. Like when they do in the doctor's, and they go like this, wrap your arm with that thing and [pumping noise]. All of a sudden this arm started to go like that. Um....And that's it. I don't like this feeling, it makes me feel like I'm gonna die! [Laugh.] I always ask if I can not do this at the doctor's.

Janet: And, um, the stuff reminded of Fridays, too. That's gonna be a tough one for me—Fridays.

Thomas: It's also a real problem for me.

Dr. Miller: Friday?

Thomas: Which is why I'd like to stay here till Saturday. I can skip one Friday. 'Cause I think Friday night's a bad time for a lot of people.

Dr. Miller: There's a story I tell about the fellow who figured out that Friday afternoon was his worst time. At the end of work he would stop off—he would stop off at the bar, have a few drinks, and then he'd have his first gram of coke, and the next thing he knew he'd be coking the whole night long. And so once we identified the problem; what he did Friday morning was give $150 for that first gram to his wife. Then she would make arrangements for the whole evening's activity, pick him up at work at 5:00 on Friday, and they'd have a whole evening for the $150 without his spending it on drugs. They'd go out to show, go to a beautiful restaurant—you know, there's a lot you can do still for $150 for an evening. And that broke the back of his, of his pattern...repeated pattern, which was always that Friday night. Some people have a Monday morning pick-me-up, start the week with the cocaine. For some it's the Wednesday, you know, Thank-God-in-the-middle-of-the-week-it's-Wednesday.

Janet: Earlier I had the thought that this would be really enough for us all to get high on tonight. That was a fleeting thought. It really was, honest to God.

Thomas: That's disgusting.

Janet: No, I know, I know...I mean, don't get greedy...there's enough for you, too.

[Laughter.]

Thomas: I'd like to....

Janet: And then if you really got desperate, you could scrape off the stuff you rubbed into the carpet last night or threw into the garbage this morning.

Dr. Miller: And you know people do it.

Janet: I've never done it, but people do scrounge for drugs...I like this mirror. [Fingering a mirror in the pile that says "cocaine" on it.]

Susan: Janet!

Janet: I'm not making fun, I'm saying that I noticed this this afternoon that I liked the mirror.

Dr. Miller: That was a recent....

Mike: I was fascinated by all the paraphernalia.

Janet: Yeah, I was amazed this afternoon—can I take this off from there, for a minute?—You ever seen anything like—that should be illegal! [She handles a pipe.]

Dr. Miller: You love the paraphernalia, that's part of the whole...mystique!...[He reaches for an ivory pipe]. Sure. Some people like this. Look at this, it's a real elephant bone or something, with a piece of jade in it.

Janet: I didn't know what the hell it was, so I picked it up. I think that's ugly.

Dr. Miller: And look at this, a real piece of junk.

Janet: Nawww....This is me! This is me! [Grabbing a base pipe from the table.]

Mike: That's a big one!

[Laughter.]

Janet: What's this one?

Dr. Miller: This is what my parents sent me. It's a cheese cutter!

[Laughter.]

Janet: You know, I didn't know what the hell it was.

Thomas: I've been curious about that ever since you set it there, too. What the hell...?

Mike: I knew it was a cheese cutter.

Dr. Miller: Huh? Did you?

Mike: I've used 'em before. To cut coke.

Janet: I'm fascinated by the things I've never seen, and that's pretty rare, because I think I've seen most of it. The pills don't even, you know, what the hell are pills, you know. I don't feel touched by them.

Dr. Miller: People have turned in every kind of pill you could imagine. [He points at the collection.]

Janet: What is *this*?

Leslie: It's a bong. It's a big bong.

Janet: Oh. I'm disappointed.

Mike: It's a trap.

Dr. Miller: So. What?

Susan: I didn't go to sleep during group tonight. Something kept me wide awake.

Dr. Miller: You didn't go to sleep tonight, that's right. And we've got more to do yet.

Mike: Night's not over.

MAKING A NEW BEGINNING

When something so large as a body of addictive behaviors is removed from a lifestyle, there remains a great emptiness. This space must be filled with new behaviors—new, healthier activities. Addiction-focused psychotherapy must not overlook the importance of building a new life and the demands that such a building process places on patients. Rebuilding a life is a challenging, even awesome experience for many people who are recovering from, or attempting to recover from, addiction. Just anticipating the work involved in making a new beginning can be overwhelming.

Dr. Miller: Well, I told you all at the beginning of our work together that we must first build a foundation. And I hope that every one of you realizes that a week of intensive psychotherapy is not an end in and of itself. The beginning was when you acknowledged that your connection with chemical substances was out of control. The next step was coming to this intensive program and allowing your system to start to balance itself. Each of you knows just how differently you feel now, at the end of one week of deep emotional work and education. I don't have to put that experience into words, because you're feeling it on the inside. You've made it through the entire week clean and sober. You see that you can put one day after another. That's what this week is about: to show you what's possible…is to show you that, in a short period of time, you can start to turn yourself around from a very serious, profound connection with even the most reinforcing of chemicals. And now you know it's possible to start feeling your body again. And you've started to feel your self-esteem building, like the flame inside is a flame now, instead of an ember in the ashes.

So now comes the really hard part. This is the day-by-day building, the series of days of building blocks you need to truly leave this connection with drugs behind. According to the statistics, the first ninety days are going to be the hardest for you. That doesn't mean that the fifth, sixth, and seventh month are going to be a piece of cake, but that you're liable to feel the strongest cravings during the first time period, so be prepared. You want to be prepared, especially during the coming ninety days, with regard to being hungry and angry and lonely and tired. Please, please, do not in any way take what I'm saying to mean that, if you get by three months, you can go out and celebrate and have a little toot or a glass of champagne. Because all the evidence indicates that if you are a three-gram-a-day person, and you hold off for four months, and you use a few lines, you can be right back to the level three grams a day; you won't be back to "only" four lines a day. It will not take the same amount of time as it did before to build up to the habit that you had before you quit. You can drag yourself back down with a vengeance.

And if you do use again, if you do fall, you've got to shake the snow off yourself and continue on down the slope. You really can't afford to take the time to beat yourself for a week or two and then further drug yourself for a week or two with remorse. Your life is on the line. And if you think your life is worth something, then it's worth putting in the effort. If you don't, if your life's cheap, then you have another alternative. We have to respect you if you choose that alternative. You have a right to do that, to go out coking, drugging, or drinking.

Keep in mind that you do have the opportunity to change for the better. One time about twenty years ago I went to study with a prominent therapist in Atlanta, Georgia. He invited me in on all of his sessions. I was sitting with him as he worked with one of his patients. He looked at me and he said, "You have a very quizzical look on your face." I said, "Yes, I do. I wonder what she is doing here? She doesn't seem to need to be here." And he said, "At this point she's here for me. For the first couple of years she was here for her." He said, "After a couple of years, she didn't need me any more. I wanted to have the pleasure of sitting with her for a couple of sessions when she didn't need me, just to enjoy her."

This time with you is a pleasure and an honor for me, because I see the beginnings of growth. I feel the hope and the excitement of healing.

You people are the tip of the iceberg. There are countless others who need to come in for help. They are the ones who are out there trying to macho it out, trying to white knuckle it, or trying to avoid the stigma of being pointed to as an alcoholic or a drug addict. So they're hiding, afraid to let anybody know, afraid that their families will find out, afraid that their business associates will find out—just like some of you are afraid. by doing what you all are doing, you're going to open the door for a lot of other people.

You represent America. Let's look at who we are here, a homemaker, a business woman, a business man, an athlete, a builder, a film editor, a scientist, a competitive skater, and others; people from all parts of the country, from Kentucky, from Texas, from Illinois, from Los Angeles, from the San Francisco Bay Area, from New York, and elsewhere. This is it, gang, this is what we're doing to ourselves. You all came here to help turn this problem around for the sake of your own lives, and as you do that, you are helping others. For that, I thank all of you.

Mike: I just hope I can someday do for somebody what you have done for me.

Dr. Miller: [Very softly.] And you can.

"My son wasn't kicked out of school for being a bad student, I just couldn't make the payments. I spent his tuition money on drugs."

7

The Honesty Tool:
A Dialogue With Dr. Richard
Louis Miller

We have seen the truth
and it is us.

(Anonymous Group Therapy Participant)

I have had the pleasure of many fascinating conversations and interviews with Dr. Richard Miller. I have included selected excerpts of these conversations below.

Author: *Let's say I have given up drugs and several weeks later I begin to feel uncomfortable. What should I do?*

Dr. Miller: Just asking the question is an example of how little most of us know about feelings. There is nothing to do about feelings except *feel* them. Feelings are transitory, just as life is. They never last forever, no matter what they are.

Author: *Suppose I don't like my feelings?*

Dr. Miller: Well, when you don't like your feelings, you are not liking yourself, for your feelings are part of yourself. Sit there and let yourself experience these feelings that you do not like. You will not die. You will just be uncomfortable and you may learn a great deal about yourself.

Author: *What is the origin of my discomfort with my feelings?*

Dr. Miller: We are taught the rules of behavior by our families and by society. As kids we are taught the yes-yes's and the no-no's. In other words, we learn what is okay and what is not okay to do. We are also taught these same yes-yes's and no-no's regarding feelings. It is okay to feel happy and to laugh. It is not okay to feel angry. Little boys are taught a different set of yes-yes's and no-no's than little girls. For boys, crying is a no-no, and for girls, yelling is a no-no. Many of us are taught to control or override our emotions rather than to express them. We are also taught that there is a time and place to express certain feelings and not others.

Is it any wonder that most of us are so uptight? After all, humans are feeling animals whose emotions are a very important aspect of their existence. Yet we are taught to hold so many of our feelings in, particularly the painful ones. So imagine that you are going through some pain related to your previous drug abuse. You have probably been taught to cover up your pain or, maybe, to do something like take a drug to get rid of it. Well, here is an opportunity to make a major step toward personal freedom. Do nothing but experience your feelings. Sit there, and close your eyes, and just feel.

Is the feeling you are having one of your no-no's? Is it a feeling that you have early on been taught not to experience? Doesn't that sound silly? To have a feeling that you are *not supposed to have*? Here I am, having a feeling that I am not supposed to have.

Author: *Should I do this with all my feelings?*

Dr. Miller: This is a good time to make a list of your personal yes-yes's and no-no's of emotions. In other words, list what feelings are okay for you to have and what feelings are not okay. Note what feelings are only okay in certain situations and name these situations. It will be useful to *just feel* with all your feelings, but begin with the feelings that you are suppressing, that are no-no's for you.

Author: *What can I do with the feeling of wanting drugs?*

Dr. Miller: Close your eyes and look at this feeling. Always remember that a feeling must have a location because it must exist somewhere. If you are unable to point to the feeling, you are probably not having a feeling, but rather you are having a thought, and calling the thought a feeling. We often confuse our thoughts and feelings. When you begin a sentence with "I feel that I am warm," you are not talking about a feeling. For a feeling is not a *that,* as in "I feel *that* I am...." A feeling statement is "I feel warm," or "I feel cold," or "I feel pressure." You see, in each case, you are following the words *I feel* with a sensation, "I feel tension." "I feel tight, warm, cold, pressure." These are sensations. "I feel that" is not a feeling. "I feel that I am doing..." That is not a feeling. It is important to distinguish your thoughts from your feelings. Remember that a feeling has a physical sensation of some sort. You can always point to a feeling:If you look for it, you will find it in your body.

Author: *I think it is critical that we continue to feel in a world that is encouraging us not to be human, not to feel. We treat ourselves like machines when we do not recognize feelings. We specialize in thinking about feelings rather than in having them.*

Dr. Miller: I agree with you. And while many chemically dependent people are drugging their feelings, many other members of our society are denying, ignoring, and stuffing away their feelings.

Author: *This is a frightening step in the evolutionary process. I think that this trend indicates that the human species is at a choice point. It can become more machinelike to survive the future, or more feeling to stay human in the future. If we become less feeling, more machinelike, we lose our humanity—humanity does not survive.... Now, once I decide to feel my feelings, can I change them without stopping the process of feeling—without turning off?*

Dr. Miller: Keep in mind that feelings are transitory, and therefore they can change and they can be changed. There are things you can do to change a feeling in addition to simply waiting for a feeling to change itself.

One way is to express your feeling. What is the sound of your feeling? Make this sound out loud. Of course, you may feel a sense of discomfort or embarrassment making the sound out loud. So what! There is no sign in the sky that says we must be 100% comfortable every time we try something new. Make the sound of your feeling out loud. And do it again and again.

Another way to change a feeling is to breathe. Breathe in and out in a way that allows your stomach to move in and out. If your clothes are tight, loosen them so they do not restrict your breathing, and then continue to breathe. Small breaths, moving your stomach in and out—small breaths, not hyperventilating. After you breathe like this for several moments, take your finger tips and begin to massage your stomach very gently. Then massage deeper and deeper into your stomach, checking for tight areas or knots. Do not move rapidly. Continue to breathe and to massage your stomach. It is very important to keep your stomach loose, for this is the area where most of us feel our uptightness or our tension. When you keep this area loose with this breathing exercise and with your finger-tip massage, your whole system will feel it.

Author: *When I do not do something to change my feelings, and, instead, I cover them up, deny them, am I hurting myself?*

Dr. Miller: Watch out! Covering over feelings, whether we do it with or without drugs, costs us a lot. Covering feelings is sometimes called "sandbagging." We have a different bag for each of the feelings that we keep inside. For example, every time we feel anger and stuff it down, it goes into our anger bag. Then one day someone says one little thing that upsets us, and we hit them with the whole bag. The more the bag is full, the harder it is to control, and that is why some people seem to walk around like a bomb ready to go off. Many people try to cover over these sandbags with drugs. This can be very dangerous. For example, when using a drug like cocaine, suspicion and paranoia are exaggerated. Combined with the anger already stuffed in the sandbag, and perhaps with a little booze as well, this can make a human being extremely dangerous.

Author: *It seems that if I use drugs not to feel, I fall prey to being controlled by those drugs—addicted—and also to being out of control— "extremely dangerous," as you say. Will this happen if I use drugs that I am not addicted to also?*

Dr. Miller: It can. One certain pitfall is the seemingly casual use of drugs other than the one or ones to which you think you are addicted. Remember, if you are a little high on pot or booze or a drug to which you are not addicted, your ability to say "no" to the drug to which you are addicted is decreased, and you may get onto your drug-using cycle again. While you are off the drug cycle, find ways to applaud yourself for your accomplishments. If you do slip or fall, you will only harm yourself further by responding with self-criticism. Use the fall as further evidence for the difficulty of your task and focus on the success you have already achieved.

Author: *Can friends be pitfalls, too?*

Dr. Miller: Yes. Friends can be pitfalls if they use drugs. And if you are quitting and they are offering you drugs, they are simply *not* your friends. Find people who won't let you make them your excuse for your drug problem.

Connect with other people who are giving up their drugs. Most drug users or drinkers I counsel associate pretty much with other drug users or drinkers, and the whole world seems to them to be full of users or drinkers. "My drug is everywhere. I just can't get away from it. There is no way I can quit." Do you hear the excuses, the rationalizations, the denial? The whole world is full of drugs! Ha! Ha!

Remember, if millions of people are using drugs, there are millions who are not. And *some* nonusers must also be hip people who enjoy life and know how to have a good time. It is essential that you find yourself a support group of nonusers. This may be Cocaine Anonymous, Alcoholics Anonymous, Narcotics Anonymous, or some other support group. You may also want to go to a public or private agency and seek professional help from a drug counselor or a professional therapist. Seeking professional help can be like shopping for anything else. You must take the time to really look around and try out several sources of help before you decide what is right for you. "Ah, that shrink was so uptight I couldn't stand it, so I took the money and I bought some drugs." All you are doing there is rationalizing your not getting help by externalizing, by blaming the shrink for your drug use. *Blaming others will simply not help you one bit.* You must *take responsibility for finding the help you need.* By the way, do not pick a professional person who wants to give you drugs to get you off drugs. All you will be doing is substituting one drug for another, and you will still be a slave to a drug. What we are looking for, what we are working toward, is freedom from drugs.

Author: *What do I do after I begin getting help?*

Dr. Miller: Keep on getting help. The continuing care, the ongoing maintenance is crucial. It took you quite a while to get connected to drugs, and it may take you quite a while to disconnect.

Author: *When I blame other people or things for my drug problem, what I am doing is trying to give away personal responsibility. This seems, again, to be an example of the surrendering of my humanity and self control. What do you think is going on when this happens?*

Dr. Miller: Addicted people grow quite accustomed to doing what mental health professionals call externalizing. That is, they justify their behavior on the basis of events outside themselves, such as, "My wife was in the hospital and then my kid broke her leg, and after being at the hospital for ten hours I just couldn't resist turning to drinks and drugs, because I needed relief." If you are an addicted person saying this, you are blaming your drug use on the fact that your wife was in the hospital and your daughter broke her leg. Well, remember, *life is full of reasons to drug yourself if you are looking for reasons.* There is always some tragedy, somebody is always sick, somebody is always getting hurt, there is usually some financial trouble going on. *If you are looking for a reason, you will always find a reason.*

One of the first things to know about most drugs is that hardly any people think they have a problem controlling their use of these drugs. Many people think that quitting drugs will be very easy, and then they try to quit again and again and again and again. Drugs give us feelings of either escape, control, or power that lead us to believe that we either can escape, control, or overpower anything. So we lead ourselves to believe that we can stop using drugs anytime we choose and stay stopped.

It is important for you to ask, "What has my relationship been with this drug? How much have I used, and how often have I used it, and in what circumstances have I used it?" Write your answers down! If you do not know what your level of consumption and your habits have been, who does?

Author: *How do I know if I really have become addicted to a drug?*

Dr. Miller: Addiction is *an uncontrollable urge.* Here are some warning signs of addiction to look for. (Alcohol is a drug, so remember that here.)

- You find yourself thinking about, or planning ahead for, the next time you are going to use drugs.
- When you have drugs and you use them, you have difficulty leaving any over for the next time.
- You find yourself associating mostly with people who use drugs, whether it be socially or at work.
- You use any excuse you can to use drugs, be it a celebration because some positive event has occurred, or relief or escape from something negative. A famous baseball pitcher who came to me said that, whenever he won a game, he used his drugs because he felt so good, and whenever he lost a game, he used them even more because he felt so bad.
- When you cannot get your drugs as quickly as you want them, you get nervous. You get an uncomfortable feeling somewhere inside. You make late night calls or trips to buy more drugs. I have heard so many stories from people about them doing the strangest things in order to get drugs in the middle of the night.
- You use money that was actually earmarked for some other purpose to buy drugs.
- Once you feel the desire for drugs, you are uncomfortable until you get some, and then, when you do get them, you do use them immediately.
- *You have tried unsuccessfully to stop.*

These are just some of the warning signs of addiction. Do any of them fit you? Do you find yourself trying to make excuses in order not to fit into some of these categories? Excuses and rationalizations are the by-products of all addictions.

Author: *These excuses and rationalizations sound like lies to me. It sounds especially terrible, this being addicted. It can happen to any-one—is that true?*

Dr. Miller: I have spent many years of my life working with addicted people and listening to the most intimate details of their lives. These people are from all walks of life. They are teachers. They are lawyers, housewives, doctors, students, taxi drivers, store owners, construction workers, and others. They are the typical Americans who started out to do some harmless recreational drinking and drug using, and, somehow, somewhere along the way, things got out of control. They became addicted. What happened then? Their relationships and their marriages were ruined. They distanced from their children. They pushed their friends and family members away. They noticed that they were spending more time with other drinkers and druggers. Addiction is far from being a harmless recreational experience. It can kill. Admitting this is the first step and the greatest tool for you to use.

Author: *This "admitting" you speak of, I think it extends to the societal level. What we need is honesty inside of each of us and among us all. Honesty is an essential tool.*

Dr. Miller: Yes, the most powerful tool of all.

PART II

THE LIFE AND TIMES
OF
ADDICTED PEOPLE

*"It is like a long one way road
into a black endless tunnel,
and there is no turning back."*

8

Introduction to Part II –
Looking at the Self

I was lost in a maze of lies.
A mirror came and found me.

(Anonymous Group Therapy Participant)

Exposure to intensive group therapy often triggers introspection, even among those who have either avoided introspection or never even considered its utility prior to therapy. This was the case for almost every participant in the group sessions scripted in this book. Chapters 8, 9, and 10 are edited-down autobiographies of a few of the group participants. These autobiographies have been included in order to provide a sense of the backgrounds of those people who arrive in Dr. Miller's groups. Although Dr. Miller's patients come from all walks of life, all age groups, all races, both sexes, and experience a broad range of addictions, their stories, and the pain behind their stories, are remarkably similar.

In telling their stories, whether in written or in spoken words, patients often weave in and out of a state of detachment. Every once in a while, the patient realizes that the life he or she is describing is not that of some stranger somewhere on the other side of the planet, but of himself or herself. Shock and pain race through his or her face and voice and body in that moment. Sometimes the feeling, the emotion, lingers on the surface for a while. Sometimes it races back into a deep hiding place almost immediately. It is the work of therapists to use the life story information of their patients, not so much because it is case history, but because it is a map into stored, buried, neglected, and denied emotion.

The therapist can coach the creation of, and then study, written autobiographies before the group therapy sessions, in order to pick out highlights, possible doorways into the conundrum of addiction. This material is valuable in gestalting a patient's addiction and all that led up to it. As you read the following autobiographies, try to identify key points and experiences in the lives of these people, points that might serve as keys to unlock doors to hidden emotional mysteries. These key points may be major events, or they may be what sound like minor events in the parade of life. Also, read, not just the lyrics, but the music—the tone and the overtures. Remember that names have been changed in these chapters in order to protect the identities of the story tellers and their friends and families.

One other note on the patient autobiography: The process of writing such an autobiography can be arduous, especially for patients who are not writers. I was able to work with the writers of the following autobiographies on a small group basis. This was a process that took several meetings and a good amount of coaching, discussion, and direction. A certain amount of training in basic writing skills was also involved, although I steered away from too much work in this area. It is important to stress to patients that, for those who are willing to write autobiographies at all, spelling and grammar is not important—these "papers" will not be graded: If this is school, it is the school of life, and the writer of the autobiography determines its outcome by choosing to live the future in a particular way. I found that I had to remind my writers of this notion on several occasions. I also had to decline requests that I write certain sentences or paragraphs for the patients, reminding them that the information and emotions about their lives that they access—discover or tap into—is purest and most powerful when they do this work for themselves. The heart, the mind and the pen must connect. The author of the autobiography contained in Chapter 10 learned this when he finally completed his writing in a jail cell and came face to face with parts of himself that he did not remember prior to this. Again, this is rich material that can be brought in for intensive work in group psychotherapy.

"At first you don't realize it's not power. It feels so much like power."

9

Autobiography of An Addict

I am a twenty-four-year-old male. My addictions are: drugs and alcohol (cocaine, marijuana, barbituates); sex and love; food. I am definitely an addicted person. I cannot have just so much of something. It has to be all or nothing.

By the time I got to tenth grade, drug use, dealing, and crime were a big part of my life and I don't know how I managed to salvage the grades to play football, which was something I always wanted to do.

And my junior year in high school started. I was supposed to go to a vocational school for trades, and when the teachers went on strike I had no idea that that school was different. But after the strike ended and I went there, my spot was filled and I had to return to high school. Well, the only classes that were open were the ones that I had no business being in because I hadn't been able to catch up, since I had skipped eighth grade. Two weeks later, I dropped out of high school and went right to work for my dad, just what I had been doing every summer anyway.

When I was eighteen years old, I met my first girlfriend. It was a big event in my life to be in love and get the attention I so much wanted.

From what I remember, I smoked pot for the first time when I was eleven years old. I think I started alcohol right around the same time. By the time I was fifteen, maybe fourteen, I was smoking pot every day and drinking pretty heavily. I was sixteen when I did cocaine for the first time. At first you don't realize it's not power. It feels so much like power. I also continued smoking pot very heavily. When I was eighteen, I started working in a big night club, and the cocaine use got more heavy. I changed clubs after a year and a half. When I was working at the first club, snorting was the only method of use, but by the time I got to the other club, my nose was so "f" up that I started free basing. Well, that got very heavy on and off, until it finally came down to wanting help, so when I was twenty-one I went to Cocaine Anonymous and tried a bit to start recovery. Needless to say I wasn't ready and only put together short lengths of sobriety. I went back and forth most of the next four years, only adding to my pain. Whenever I stayed away from cocaine I was still drinking and smoking pot, until it came to my family's attention that there was definitely a problem. I had been smoking cocaine again in mass quantities for a couple of months, and then I came to Dr. Miller, where I am now. I sit here writing this autobiography with thirty-one days clean from cocaine and twenty-six days clean and sober.

I was eighteen when I moved in with Cathy. And I never wanted to hurt anyone. But by staying in this relationship for five years I was only hurting myself. With four years of heavy drug use and some periods of good sobriety in between, I was in a bigger relationship with drugs than with a woman. During this time there were many events and crisis that definitely overshadowed any of the good events. There wasn't much going on with my family; everyone seemed to be going their own way. Then my dad had this idea to start a small business, and when I couldn't handle it I just didn't ask for any help. I failed. I actually failed. I went to college for the first time and played football. I was feeling really good about myself, and all drug using stopped. I played football with a close friend and fellow addict. The support was great. It was good to feel good about myself after the business had failed. Even my relationship with Cathy was going great. And then, boom. Three days before our first game a 300-pound kid crushed in my knee and there was no more football.

I didn't tell the people in the hospital or the doctor that I was an addict, and I got plenty of morphine. I knew then I would use (drugs) when I got out and I did, but I picked myself back up again and again started going to 12-step meetings—CA, AA, and NA. Since I wasn't very mobile for a while, the business was totally taken away from me. I was feeling like a complete failure now. My drug using was very heavy and sickening. I got thrown off my new job because of my attitude. Then I went to Boise, Idaho, on a rather large project. Things were going very well, and the learning was great. But I got sent home from there for reasons I believe now were beyond my control.

Then the crisis hit with my dad's business, and things went really bad. I went through the final break-up with my girlfriend. The rejection from her was bad enough. And then my dad would not stick up for me, and I felt totally abandoned, so then I went on a hell of a bender of using, and my life really fell apart. I spent a week in a hospital rehab. Now I have been coming to Dr. Miller for six months. I have to deal with what is going on with me right now to recover. I have to believe that I should not regret the past nor shut the door on it. But I am living for the future and I am really trying my best, honestly, going to any length to stay clean and sober. I have had too much recovery taught to me to give up now. So God bless you all and please pray for me!!!

"It has been a long run."

10
Making and Unmaking an Addict

I am a thirty-four-year male, raised in a ghetto in New York, with four brothers and one sister. My father died from his alcoholism. My mother is still a practicing co-dependent.

My addiction is also my inability to ingest alcohol or other mind-altering substances and still function effectively. The chemical imbalance in my brain clouds my judgment, and the result is insane behaviors motivated totally by the drugs to get more drugs.

I see my addiction to drugs and alcohol as just another way of mine for making me feel better. I have many compulsive behaviors. I have not let sugar and caffeine destroy my life like drugs have, although I still catch myself and occasionally submit to these simpler addictions, too. I also find myself running away from unpleasant tasks by taking a coffee break, eating, listening to music, watching TV, going somewhere, doing some less difficult task, spending money, making love, sleeping, any diversion from the reality at hand. My addiction has brought me to my knees before my God. He is the only one who can keep me sober. I thank God daily for allowing me to work through all my difficulties and never giving me more than I can handle one day at a time. I thank God for making me a cocaine and alcohol addict, and giving me the chance to really live.

It has been a long run. I grew up in a house that was about 120 years old. I remember lying in my bunk bed and being able to see outside through a hole in the boards by the window. The house was in very bad repair, and my father always did a low-quality job on any repair he did. The house was a two-storey with three bedrooms, front porch, two rear sheds. Our house was brown in color. I remember how good I felt when I made the honor roll. I remember being Robin Hood in a school play. I remember my father getting us out of school in the middle of the day to take us to the movie "Flubber." I remember my fourth-grade teacher pulling me from my chair during the art portion of the class, taking me to the window, holding up my drawing, and screaming at me in front of the class because my tree didn't look like the trees outside. I turned around and my friends were laughing, so I started to cry.

My first encounter with death was at age thirteen. On May 11th my grandfather died, I was very sad because everyone else was, I told my mother I would never go to another funeral as long as I lived. I hated it when people saw me crying and hugged me. I was so humiliated. My father died two years later on May 7th. I was forced to go to his funeral, but I refused to believe that my father had died. There were many tragedies in my life. My father's death at age fifteen, my sister being beat by her husband, my younger brother being hit by a train and losing his right arm and leg, my girlfriend of six years running off with my sister's husband.

I have unfinished business with: my dad for leaving me alone to learn all about life with no man to help me; my mother for not making him go to the hospital before he was so far gone and also for letting us kids walk all over her; my sister for the way she scared me as a child; my father for never being there even when he was alive; my brothers for leaving home and never coming back without telling us or even acting like you have a little brother; my parents for not keeping us together as a family unit and setting a good example on how to have different opinions and still remain friends and not to isolate loved ones. I have unfinished business with the church because I opened the envelope and took out the money for church and spent it on candy, then didn't go to church and lied to my mother about it; and to my brother for the way I acted like a fool when I said that you probably picked that book out of the trash when I later found out you bought it for me, I'm sorry; with my dad for not allowing me to have a bicycle like the other boys. I felt like there was something wrong with me in his eyes that I needed to be protected or I was incapable of riding a bike without getting hurt.

I always felt self-conscious when I talked, entered a room. I have always felt that I was never good enough. I had to only let out certain facts about me until I could fix me or just avoid the people that could expose my shortcomings and my weak sides that a real man doesn't have.

I received no awards in high school. It was the most embarrassing when I had to go to school with my dad and he told them that he read an article on New York teachers. It said that 95% of them were crazy.

My father died in my second year of high school. Then I was also busted twice for stealing cars, so my mother moved us out of the city. I spent the next few years wasted on glue, beer, acid, or whatever I could find. I really didn't pay much attention to what my mom said because I was going into the service and I would have a new start. I could be anyone I wanted to be.

At the age of eighteen I joined the Air Force, and on January 3, 1974, I left Buffalo for Lackland AFB in Texas. The next place I was sent was to Biloxi, Miss. Keesler AFB. I was to attend twenty-nine weeks of classes to become an Avionics Communications Specialist (Radio Repairman). I think it was in June of '74 I received an emergency phone call from Red Cross. It was my brother Jim. He told me my brother Bob had been hit by a train, and that I was to catch a flight to DC where he would meet me and we would drive to Buffalo together. When we got to the hospital my brother was awake and was in intensive care, he had lost his right arm and leg and he wanted to show it to me, I was so sad and angry at myself for not staying home to watch over him. Over the next fifteen years I returned home only six or seven times. I finished Air Force school at the top of my class, and I knew it was up to me to make it because one day I would have to take care of everybody. I was stationed at Travis AFB. I became very proficient at my job. I became airman of the month. I met a real nice girl that I tried to manipulate and she went out on me and found another man. I bought a Corvette when I was eighteen and I thought I was it. I started smoking pot and did a little acid, and always had beer in the refrigerator. I moved off base and found the party crowd. I became very antiestablishment, although I never continued my stealing ways. I didn't have another serious relationship until 1977. Until then I just would have sex with the loose woman who didn't want anything except sex. I became very bored with this lifestyle. I got a DWI in 1975.

When I got out of the service in 1977, I stayed in Fairfield and got into construction as a carpenter. I met Gail and moved in with her as a roommate. This was soon changed. I didn't have credit, so Gail showed me what to do and also about a checkbook. I made the money, and she managed it. This relationship ended when I went back to Buffalo and when I called her on New Year's Eve. She wasn't home, and I later found out she went to a party at a friend's with another friend of mine, and they all three went back to his house until the next day. I didn't know to believe the worst or what. Eventually this got to me, and she moved out.

About a month later I met Sally in a bar called Thompson's Corner. We were both drunk, so she went home with me. We fell in love, and about three weeks later she moved up from LA to move in with me. Eight months later we drove up to Lake Tahoe and got married. We bought a house and worked very hard to pay the bills and save some money. On December 31, Sally hit a $25,000 jackpot in Tahoe. Our life started going crazy after that. I became more and more insecure so I turned into an egotistical workaholic who would always brag about how much I made without really finishing high school. Sally started to build resentments, because I told her she was gaining weight and that I didn't want her looking at black men. It cut me down. I was very insecure about my ability to keep a woman at this point, and I have always read that black men have large penises, so I felt this could be my woman problem. How humiliating. The weekend before Halloween that year, Sally stayed out late and went to bed with some guy she had met at a bar; she said he treated her nice. I was more hurt than I had ever been. I got very angry and I slapped her and called her slut and other names. I told her to get out, she told me she'd made a mistake and that she would make it up to me. I told her I would forgive her and we would go on, everyone makes a mistake and I won't ruin our marriage over this. I never let her live it down. I was always accusing her of something. There were so many lies. Sally is an alcoholic and an addict also. She was doing exactly as I thought, I found out from her friend indirectly. I couldn't trust anyone. Why didn't anyone tell me. I didn't want to live without her and I couldn't live with someone who had treated me like that. I had to kill myself, and I would do it with drugs. I didn't have the guts. That would be quitting, and I knew I was going crazier by the day.

I was hallucinating and crawling around on the floor because I knew someone was in the house trying to get me. I hated myself for not kicking that guy's ass that she went to bed with, but I was so ashamed that I didn't want anyone else to find out. They already knew. It's her, not me. She missed out on the best thing that ever happened to her, me. Most days I really believe that.

Sally finally moved out because she couldn't get any sleep with me always asking her questions all night, and I wouldn't stop doing drugs. I went into treatment on December 7th and on December 10th Sally came to visit me and told me that she had filed for divorce. December 10th is my birthday. Why was she hurting me like this? I left the program and went back to doing drugs. On December 30th my brother Jim came out to see what was going on. He told me later I was going in a program or he would have me committed. I went through my first week with Dr. Miller. After that I knew I needed to make all of these changes, and with all the great new friends I had made at Dr. Miller's it would be easy.

I went back to Virginia with my brother for one month. When I returned, I found that a lot of my old friends had been using. I knew that if I saw them use I would want to also. I stopped calling them.

I decided I could control drinking without help and not let it become a problem. Just an occasional glass of wine with dinner. I would never have to use coke again if I make the necessary changes in me. I went drug or alcohol free until that April.

Sally had told me all through our marriage that she'd never had an orgasm. I began to take this very personal. I had to show her that I was capable. I really had to show me that I was capable. So I went to bed with her. She still didn't have one, and I felt like scum for doing what I did.

At the time I was using, I used one ounce of cocaine every five days and then slept for one day and would stuff as much food as I could in me before I got to my dealer, which was about 45 minutes away.

I felt a sort of high feeling even before I would do the drugs. It was as if I was getting the high from memory. The feeling that I had was one of extreme discomfort. My temples were pulsing and my sides below my ribs had pressure pushing out.

My life today is filled with much learning and less confusion, although there is still a lot. I am learning on a daily basis how to accept those little things that I would spend so much energy trying to change. I have the most difficulty when it comes to accepting the ones I love the most. I now recognize that there is a higher power in my life whom I choose to call God. I pray every morning and night for strength and guidance to do his will. I love myself today. I believe everything happens for a reason. I would not have been given this new way to see life if I had lived my life any other way.

I am a grateful addict and alcoholic. My life is getting better every day. I believe that God will never give me a situation that He and I can't handle together. I now realize all of the choices that I have in my life and I now know I make them for myself. I can wake up in the morning and decide to commit suicide or to live my life doing the best I can at all times. God gives me power to do so. I chose the latter. My God always shows me the right way to go. I'm the one who would not choose suicide. I will always be thankful to Dr. Miller and his staff for heading me in the right direction and being there when I realized that my old way just did not work.

My career goals are to build my business. I will finish school for real estate and get my license. I will use my license to prepare me for my broker's license in two years. I will build a very successful business combining my contractor's and my broker's license. I would like to go together with my brother and his wife on a national franchise.

My emotional life goals are to develop an attitude that allows others the chance to become all they can be and in return the same for me. I will do this by acceptance of others' ways and thoughts as their own. I will learn to be unafraid of social situations that might cause me humiliation. I will learn to accept criticism, being thankful for the opportunity to improve. I will learn not to expect special consideration from anyone. I will learn to remain open-minded to others because everyone has something to teach me. I will no longer indulge in self-pity. I will not allow my feelings to be easily hurt. I will learn to come out of myself to experience all that the world has to offer me each new day.

My dreams are very different now from when I was a boy, or even from a year ago. My dreams are now of a serene and spiritual nature. I no longer see a specific place or point I want to be at in my life—it's more like a state of mind or consciousness. My dreams are for inner strength and a conscious contact with God.

I have goals to be an influential man in the business and political community in which I live. I no longer believe that my past can hold me back in the future. Today I begin a new life. I can greet this day with love in my heart. I feel that my life experiences can be of great value to people. My recovery is a miracle. I am living proof that anything is possible with God in my life. I ask God for some type of crisis in my life every day so I can always be reminded of my lack of control in this life, and that there is nothing that God and I can't handle and still continue to grow. My dream is to really get to know myself from the inside out.

I now see life as a wonderful gift that I received as a child. I see my purpose now as one of a student. I have been given an opportunity to see everything in a new way and the beauty of it all is at times overwhelming. I once thought of my insanity as a curse. I now view myself as crazy and rely on it to give me the courage and strength I need to do the things my God tells me. My God is also crazy by human standards, and people's opinions don't bother him, he still finds a way to love everybody. I can say today that I love everybody and I will make mistakes and forgive myself as I forgive others. Life is for living. It's just that simple.

"It will be a long goodbye."

11

The Long Run

This is the story of my addiction to alcohol and cocaine, and of the path my life has taken leading to my recovery. As I've become more and more sober over the last year, I see my life as a long binge, a run for twenty-plus years, a party that did not stop, a desperate, mad journey that led me to the edge of life and to the other side. I would like to chronicle the events, philosophies, and actions that pulled me ever deeper into the horror that my alcoholism and drug addiction became. I will attempt to describe the bottom as I can remember it and the light that has shown me the way out. I will also show my life today and what it takes to keep me in today.

When I was a kid I was big in size for my age, and very full of energy, always oversized, with a lot of get up and go. I worked a great deal of my free time. I was mowing lawns and washing dishes in a restaurant when in fourth grade. I remember that I worked when other kids were playing. I felt different because I was more adult and responsible than the rest of the kids, and also because of my size. At school I was popular but never the best, smart but never brilliant. I liked sports but never was a star. On the streets I liked adventure but never got into real trouble. I really liked going to the mountains with my family when we lived in Colorado. Fishing trips in high mountain streams were the only time I was close to my dad. At home he seemed distant and unavailable, but he loved the outdoors and I felt a part of his life there. I wanted to please him, and he only praised me for working or for my interest in hunting and fishing.

I was independent and ran my own schedule from an early age. I did not fight with my parents and for the most part had little to do with my brother or sister. My mom loved me dearly and would over-mother me if I let her. She seldom got a chance, for I was always gone. I worked too much and could have spent more time being a kid. I believed the real world was adult and the kid things I knew were not as important. I did not see that there was trouble ahead in growing up too fast. I was a good boy and a good student, but I was already living in two worlds. I was sure of myself with adults, in business, and at work, but I had trouble with my self-esteem around other kids and being cool and social. I never could fit into any one group.

As I got older, I kept this up. A good student, a good athlete, a good worker, but also a fuck-off and a street rowdy. I felt I had a lot going but could not be the best in any one area. Few people could keep up with my dynamo life that covered so many bases. But I cheated myself by not applying myself fully in any one area. I needed to be really good at something to prove my worth and that never happened. I was trying to be a lot of different people all at once so as not to come to grips with myself.

I worked after school and between sports. I worked the three to twelve shift as a waiter and busboy in a restaurant in my junior and senior years. Quite a load. I bought a new fast motorcycle and starting leaning to the rebel side. I was still a good student and athlete, but now I was also angry and wanted to become a crazy man. Little did I know that I was a very unusual person that was capable of the wildest. I saw an image of myself as a strong tough guy that took what he wanted. I thought this would hide the soft, sensitive, fearful side that was always in the background. I worried that I could not fit into the cool grove. I worried that I was not sure of myself. I was fighting the honesty and sensitivity that would be my most special assets. No one else seemed to be mixed up. I felt something was wrong with me. I became more and more angry; I was not who I wanted to be; I did not know who I wanted to be. The cream of the crop had the advantages before the rest. I saw that life was not fair. I saw hard work was not rewarded. I found alcohol.

From the start I could drink more than the rest. I became increasingly wild and crazy, and angry. Alcohol rang my bell. The successful men I knew drank. This was the trademark of the rough; alcohol separated the men from the boys. I liked it, everything about it. My friends and I would drink a fifth of scotch or a case of beer each and then see how fast our cars or motorcycles could go. How wild we could get. How loud we could yell. Parties didn't start until we got there. The party did not end until everything was consumed, till no one could walk anymore. I was the last person standing. I knew then that booze was the answer for me. It made my insecurities go away. It gave me the guts to do the wildest things. I could ride a motorcycle standing on the seat with one hand at night with the lights off at one hundred mph. No shit.

I met a girl, Mary, the belle of the class. I didn't hang out with girls at school; my world was booze, sports, and work. I think that I was too self-conscious and afraid to approach girls I liked. Somehow I went by her house on my motorcycle. She went with me; she was tired of the good little boys. I was a mover, a wild man; she liked it. She drove me crazy from the start. I never really had any other relationship; we were seventeen and juniors in high school. We never billed ourselves as a big love affair. Things just worked out. She was intelligent and sensitive, she was very pretty, she would take chances or let me take them. She was from a large family, as I soon found out, of heavy drinkers. Five brothers and five sisters and a wild man father who was a great family man and an Irishman drunk. I now know that the alcoholism she grew up with set our relationship in concrete. She was looking for an alkie to hook up with and didn't know it. She was always in control but wanted someone who wasn't. Someone who could be crazy and take the blame. For eighteen years our love developed into a horrible alcoholic scenario. At first, we talked and lived and trusted and worked together. We seemed to be as close as any two people could be. We worked our way through college and travelled around the world. We complemented each other. We were willing to grow mentally, we took chances with our lives, we did many things most people never dream of doing. The acid test of a relationship is travel, and yet we were closest on the road, with backpacks and little money. We were hard-working middle-class kids with high drive and potential. Neither of us had much confidence in ourselves and we did not recognize our assets.

Only after many years did we start to realize that we had much more going for us than the rest. But by then it was too late to reap the joys. By then king alcohol had overtaken us. It is a terrible shame that a couple with so much togetherness and love could be torn apart by the horrors of alcoholism.

I hung out with several heavy drinkers throughout high school and into college. Mary was always close and often with me as my friends and I drank. Night stocking in a grocery store, school all day, and a fifth of scotch after school every day. Wild parties and a lot of fear. Vietnam was happening.

Several of my friends were very intelligent, sensitive, and rebellious. They led me to a philosophy of hate against the society, into drugs and into the sixties. Fuck the war was really fuck anyone who wants to control us. Fuck anyone at all. We wanted it *all*, and we wanted it *now*. We were wine philosophers. We did not consider LSD and pot to be drugs, and few of us had heard of cocaine. At this time, Buddy came home from

Vietnam on leave. This was the beginning of my first serious alcohol trouble. After drinking for two days, Buddy and I shot out ten thousand dollars worth of windows. We got caught; I lost my job and fell into a horrible depression. My grades failed, I was called up for the draft, I lost all my power, and I drank more. Mary stayed. I flunked the draft. My hearing was bad from shooting too many guns and riding too many motorcycles without a helmet.

I started back to school. I went to Sacramento State College in business. I got a heavy job, sweating for eight hours a night, getting two hours of sleep a night, and still I drank every night or morning when I got off work. On weekends we did LSD or mescaline and drank. I thought that these drugs were opening my doors of perception. Actually, I was blowing my doors wide open with dynamite. I *did* change many perceptions of the world. I came to see our bullshit society for what it was, and to see the simple things for the beauty they were. Music, love, adventure, caring for others, nature, and the deep mind were opened to me. I now believe I would have gotten to this higher consciousness without drugs.

My anger became more directed at society and its unfairness. My inner hate of myself, manifested by my continued use of alcohol, lashed out at the world. I set myself apart from the world around me and could not see the good in the bad. I isolated myself. My high self-esteem and power dropped. I could not move. I became trapped in an intellectualism that would not let me go. I was so hateful of the world and its ways that I would not enter it. Although I could, at an early age, function in society so well, I became incapacitated and eventually so full of fear that I could not function at all. I was disgusted with myself. I needed to move, to accomplish, to drive, to see, and I could not. I needed challenge, but was afraid to go after it. I was caught in a horrible mental trap. I know now that the alcoholism was a great deal of the cause. I was living an alcohol depression cycle, full of fear and terribly low self-esteem. I felt I was weak and had no guts. My system of depression and hating myself through hating the world became a life theme. My friends added fuel to this system, Mary agreed. I knew I was right. The blues became a way of life, and always present were my drugs and alcohol.

Every year or so I would gather up my power and do something. During these times, I felt very close to major success. I started working for myself, painting houses. I had long hair and a beard and a philosophy that would not let me move into society. I also had a booze and drug habit that required my own time schedule. The real truth about why I decided to be my own boss is not totally clear. I did hide behind the drugs and booze issue; however, I was well suited to working for myself. I am a self-starter and have high drive. I *could* have eventually carried my dream of big success through if it hadn't been for the ever-increasing effect of alcohol. I bought houses and remodeled them. I hustled and ran things well. I understood the way of profit. I still believed in higher anti-money principles, but I felt that *I* was working against the world and its evil: I was justified in winning my battle any way I could. I had "deals" on equipment, paint, lights, lumber, labor. If I could not buy the things I wanted under the table, stolen, or at tremendous discount, I would trade drugs for them. Many acquaintances wanted to know what it was like to be free-wheeling. I knew, so I would show them. I would give a light salesman one gram of coke for one thousand dollars worth of lights. I had a deal and a way with everything. I paid cash to my employees or I gave them coke. I didn't pay taxes because there were no records. I worked the system to its hilt. I wrote my own rules. I could not see any morality in society. I believed I could do anything that I had the guts to do. Money came and went. I took chances. Drug deals, guns, quick buys, large contracting jobs. I made my own hours, I spent more and more time in bars. I was crying the blues, with twenty thousand dollars in my pocket and a pistol in my coat. I was a crazy man. I stayed up all night on coke and drank all day. I lived in fear of the law or taxes catching up with me. I felt things forever closing in. I did fewer and fewer things that I like to do.

My dad died. I was devastated; I would not accept his death. I wanted to prove myself to him and now it was too late. I wanted to know him better and he was gone. I started drinking and meant it. This was my turning point into full blown alcoholism. I went from a partier to a serious drinker. I hurt badly inside. When I was alone, I would cry. This lasted for years; I missed him terribly, I still do. I could not stop drinking when I started. I felt better drunk. When I was drunk, I did not have to be afraid of business, I did not have to feel the pain of my dad's death, and I did not have to feel remorse, although my actions were getting worse and worse all the time. I could not explain to Mary why I could not control myself or do something about my drinking. I could not face the issues of my life.

I still worked very hard but got nowhere. I sabotaged myself at every turn. If things were getting better in some area, I would make sure that it didn't last. I hated myself. I started to wish I was dead, I started to seriously doubt myself and my abilities. I could not stand what I had become. I became more and more involved with coke. A long-time friend who is a smuggler and hit man for a San Diego mob would come by with a ten-pound bag of top-of-the-line coke. We would snort grams at a time, huge quantities of booze and coke. We had money; we were going to win big. Big coke plans, big delusions. Extra cool, in the know, on top of the world. I saw a way to win quickly; I thought money and success would fix things. I was so close, when I won at their game then I would return to the person I really was. I was playing the come-line. I would win big or lose, no middle for me.

Mary waited. We had a baby boy. She did not know the danger I was in. She had no idea of the chances I was taking or the game I was really playing. I was putting everything on the line all the time. The race was on; I was under terrible pressure. The contracting became more and more intense, and business became hard. The recession was here, and I got caught. I was so close but so far away from success; I knew I could not win. The fear and pressure were overwhelming. I could not tell Mary that I could not stop and that I could not go on. My drinking was out of control. I got caught for my first drunk-driving offense.

During this time I became very close to my son. He was with me a great deal of the time. Mary worked and was busy most of the time. I liked taking care of him. We went to my jobs together and all over town. Even today I feel very connected to him, and we know each other well. He has seen me at my worst. I think he knows what I went through. My dreams failed me; I had nothing much left of who I once was. I spent the time taking care of the house and my son. I hoped that this was contributing to the family, because I knew I was tearing it apart with my drinking.

I got another drunk driving, and within months, one more. I was in real trouble now. I got lucky in the sentencing and was able to pay one before they found out about the second (actually, the third) DUI. I did some time, washed county cars, went to classes. I started to realize I had a problem with booze. I knew that I fit all the requirements to be an alcoholic. I did nothing about it except more drinking. Mary threatened to throw me out if I didn't stop. I went to a drug and alcohol clinic. I learned a lot about how alcohol works there. I had no trouble quitting drinking. I saw the therapist and was doing well in their program. But I was snorting one-half to one gram of coke a day. They didn't ask me about my coke habit, and I didn't tell them.

I kept snorting coke. My life did not get better. Mary seemed to drift further and further away. She could not be nice to me. Everything I did, good or bad, was wrong. She gave me no help, she went further into her job and friends. She did not want to talk to me or be with me. I did not drink for a year and a half, but was increasingly heavy into coke. Everything I made was spent on it. I couldn't control the amount; I became so compulsive that I would do anything for another line. I had no regard for my commitments or my family. Everything was second to coke. I would use an eight ounce during the day. For a while I could still work; soon I had to plan work around when I was not too high. Mary did not know how bad it was. She saw me only getting stranger, and she kept pulling away. I could see everything I cared for falling apart before my eyes. The fear and pain were overwhelming. I could not stand it. She hated me, and I hated me. Nothing was right in any area. I could not stop. I blamed everyone and everything. I thought of death every day. I associated with low life; I became low life.

I lost sight of all the good that was left in me. I started to believe that I *was* a *bad* person; the only side of me that I could see was the bad. Mary hated me so much that she seemed to be aggressively trying to hurt me. She seemed to feed on my weakness and pain. She treated me worse than I treated myself. I always keyed in on her feelings, and I could not handle her hate and rejection of me. She did not come home any longer on weekends or several nights a week. I stayed at home with my son and feared the time she would come home and find me high again. I slept for two years on the sofa. I was a piece of trash and believed it. I started having trouble hustling coke. My credit was wearing out. I got too high and it wore on the insane people I was with. The ugly world of drugs, and money, and threats, and lying and cheating was my life. I was surrounded by gross situations on every side. The world was ugly and fearful. I started to believe that people lived like that. I was involved in behavior and with people I would not ever before have anything to do with. I closed my doors to others and lived alone; I was so terribly lonely. I would drive somewhere alone and break down and cry, I would scream, I would have to stop driving. I felt the end was near, I thought of suicide all the time, and death was very close.

I started to drink again; I had to come down from the coke. I was staying up for days at a time. After two to three days of coking, my body would wear out, I needed to come down. I went back to alcohol. It didn't matter anymore, I knew I could not stop the terror, I just wanted to hide. I started stopping in the same old bars, and within a very short time I was drinking like before, but worse. I could not tell how much to drink. Sometimes one drink would get me drunk; sometimes it would take twenty. The depression of alcohol, together with the paranoia of coke, made me real weird. I was getting dangerous. Carrying a gun, ready to kill someone. I was afraid, and my delusions and fantasies and fears were becoming real. I wanted to strike out, but there was no one to attack. I did not care about anything except my son. I was going insane, the world was closing in on me, I was at a breaking point. I had held it off for many years, but this was the end and I knew it.

I could not stand the hate Mary was throwing at me any longer. Things had come to a head; she was ripping me apart with terrible accusations. My business was broke; I snorted forty thousand dollars in one year. I had no assets left, no will, my family was falling apart, the IRS was after me. I got my fourth drunk driving.

Things were very surrealistic around me. I was numb, I could not stand anymore, I wanted to die for real. I was planning my death; it was just a matter of time. I pulled my 44 magnum out and put it in a dealer's mouth, pulled the hammer back, and he just said, "Do it, I don't care." I should have. A friend came over and I pointed a loaded shotgun at him but could not kill him. I ran and hid but nothing would stop the fear and pain. I reached the point where alcohol and coke did not kill the pain anymore, but I could not stop. It was a nightmare that was real. I found terror. I do not remember things or days; they just melt together in pain. This is very painful to relive. It hurts to write it.

People started telling me that I needed help. After a three-day binge, a half-ounce later, and much wine, I knew that I would kill myself. I reached out finally. I knew I might only have one chance left. I called a person I had talked to weeks before, as a way to make my mother feel better.

This person knew I was serious. I did not believe anyone could help me. I did not believe in help, but I was so devastated that I surrendered. I was willing to try anything. I came to Dr. Miller's program and met with his staff. I knew I could trust them. They told me the truth. They would not back down. They won my respect. I decided to listen to Dr. Miller, something I had never done for anyone. He knew I was dying, and he said he would stick with me if I would try. I could not believe anyone would give so freely as that staff. I needed their help and accepted it. I went to their program. I was so spun out that I could not stop the fear and pain. My wife had left me, I was barely alive. I knew that this was probably the last chance I would have to stay alive. I was not sure I wanted to live, however.

At Dr. Miller's I felt at home. It was where I needed to go. He said that, if I let go, I could live again, that something would put my life together, if I could trust. I know that something put these special people and this special place in my life at this time of need. Richard Miller was the leader of the group. He was my friend from the start. I felt that I had known him all my life. I could communicate with him without speaking, he radiated love and trust. He would lend his strength, and he said he would take a chance on me. He seemed to know my pain. I trusted them all totally. I have never known a man with so much courage. I met his wife, Angela, a therapist and seminar leader there. I looked in her eyes and saw trust and love. She held my hand and put something of herself back into me. All of these special people did much more for me than their jobs required. I know I found true humanity and love. The tiny bit of beauty that was so much a part of me was relighted. I was being loved back to life.

I was determined to do whatever it took to stay sober, but I did not think it would work. I did not want to make the many changes that were to come up, but I could not go back. I was forcing myself to go forward. I had always thought that I was in touch with feelings; I came to realize that I would let my feelings in and then black them out with alcohol and drugs. I found out that sobriety is learning to live with my feelings. I found out that there were many things inside me that had been buried for years that I had not dealt with, there were things about me that were part of me before I was drinking and needed to be dealt with. I needed to learn a new way of dealing with feelings without drugs. I have to say good-bye to drugs. It will be a long good-bye.

I had never realized the real reason in me through all this insanity. I had no idea that I was so sick. I needed to learn a new way to live. I wanted the pain to stop, and I wanted to feel good again, a feeling I did not remember. It took months to ease up on myself, but as time went on I could see that, as I worked on myself, I was making progress. I set up a regular system of Twelve Step meetings and therapy.

Dr. Miller told me to write an exercise plan. Now I exercise every day. I jog in the morning for twenty minutes. I found that I need to return to the physical person I once was. I play racquetball, and this releases much aggression I have built up during the day. The main benefit for me is the aerobic effect. My spirits are always lifted after exercise. I feel better about myself, and this is the goal. I have a tool in exercise: It helps to release the anxieties and troubles. I am better able to do the strenuous things I love as my body gets stronger.

I spend time every morning stretching. For me this is a great start for the day. I can loosen the tired and worn parts of myself. I also can use this time to focus on myself. The stretching puts me in touch with me. I feel better after stretching. After I stretch, I spend time meditating. I have worked out a system that helps me let go. I am just getting into this area, and I can see many positive results. I plan to explore meditation for myself in the years to come. This helps me to center myself. I can stop the pressures and demands that are put on me and that I put on myself. I can clear the slate; I can go out of my space and take a breath. I can come back with a new outlook, and this helps me function in my high-pressure world. I can deal with the day better. Meditation also feels good after I do it.

I have found that eating and diet are major influences on my state of being. I am big, and too much food is another way of not dealing with things. I can eat and numb myself. The things I eat can cause me to feel up or down. I am conscious of this cause-and-effect scenario and try to pay attention to it.

All of my "program" leads me to the belief today that I *can* do something about the way I feel. I can do this by changing the way I perceive the world. I can have freedom by controlling how I feel. I don't have to let things or people dominate or own me. I want to return to myself and real feelings that are not composed of winning or fighting. I want to know serenity and have it near me. This will take many years of hard work, but it is exciting, it is what I want, it feels good to align myself with the universe around me. I do not want the pain anymore. I know that I make my own pain, and that only I can make me feel. I can choose to feel good over bad. The bad in the world is how I want to perceive it, the world affects me the way I want it to. I need to learn more about this, and I will.

I am writing this from a jail cell. I am doing time for my last DUI. The best day in my past is not as good as the worst day in here, sober. I can get through this and can make it positive. I look forward to running my new commercial fishing boat off Tomales Point in the fog and heavy seas. I want to dive for abalone, to feel the wind whipping the ocean against my face. I want to be here for my son, and I am. I want to make my business work and become a sane, well-organized operation, and that is happening. I am trying to live one day at a time. I am learning exciting things, I am moving again, answers are being revealed. I am free today, I do not have to drink or use drugs today. I choose not to. I can meet my fears head on. The world is starting to open up for me. I feel younger. I have found a way out of alcohol and drugs; the way out is taking care of myself. A small price to pay for life.

"What drives you to use is inside you."

12

The Poetry of the Struggle

In every struggle with the self, there is poetry waiting to be spoken and song waiting to be sung. Perhaps the tension between the competing drives of destruction and survival triggers the creative impulse. This chapter contains poems and songs written by group therapy participants. Poetry says some things so much more clearly than prose.

BEAM ME UP, SCOTTY!

(Anonymous Group Therapy Participant)

When things are going really shitty
I like to pout and look full of pity.
I sometimes laugh at my position
I want support, I want you to listen.
I think as I write, I want you to fix it—
Listening isn't enough - I want a quick exit.
I must be afraid of settling down
I don't want a commitment—
I like fooling around.
I bitch a lot about my situation
I could be worse off, check out our nation.
Today I am angry and life can really suck
I feel jerked around, I just need a good fuck.
Only God can send the message I need.
I trust his doings—but I am tired
of life's screwings!

I can't believe how disgusting
I can be—at least I am not using
and I am chemical free.
So if my language is poor and my mannerisms disgusting
I am still proud and my brain
isn't combusting.
I amaze myself at how I have endured
I just have to remember my disease
is never cured.
I must always remember my times of pain
There was nothing solid in my life
There was nothing to gain
My gratitude to myself is my #1 high
For I am so healthy and so very *alive*
I may cry too much
But I probably only need the
Love of the human touch.
What a simple cure for such
A deadly disease.
Sometimes just a big hug will
Put me at ease.
To all that have stood by me
In times of good and bad,
To all who helped when I was
really sad,
I will forever hold you in my heart
And never forget your support
You gave before I fell apart.
I don't do drugs and staying
Clean now is my game.
Thanks for listening to my candid
Rhyme—
It is an uncut version, thank you for
Your time!

TOO MANY TIMES

(Anonymous Group Therapy Participant)

There's a great many times
That we've shown ourselves
The awesome things
That remain on the shelves.
Then again and again
We've always said
That life without each other
would be as if dead.

(Chorus)

What can I be
You can tell me
Where I can go to the next time.
You just let me know
And I will show
For the last and final time.

(Chorus)

There's too many times
That we let our love fall.
Too many times
That we passed the ball.
Then again and again
What had remained
Was life on this Earth
Just barely sustained.

(Repeat Chorus)

There's times I've been happy
Times I've been sad
There were many times
When I knew what was bad.
There's a key for us all
To open the door.
You need only know
What you're looking for.

(Repeat Chorus)

COKENDERS POEM

(Anonymous Group Therapy Participant)

While looking for a card, I found it very hard,
One that could be bought, just didn't have the thought.
I thought I'd take the time, to write this little rhyme,
The problem with the coke, was really not a joke.
The ending of the week, my outlook was quite bleak,
I finally made the call, and packed to make the haul,
up to Wilbur Springs, to try to come out clean.
The point of this week's trip, to save a sinking ship,
The program they had there, I heard was more than fair,
It had a group of folks, who knew it was not a hoax,
to lose your soul and power, for years and months and hours.
The drugs that took control, were covering up my soul,
The program was coke-enders, there's really no pretenders.

It's run by a sharp staff, who still know how to laugh,
It's headed by Doc Miller, he's really quite a pillar.
He works with his great crew, to try to make us new,
It started out with Andy, who really was quite handy
at talking on the phone, you know you're not alone,
Angela and her charts, we learned some funky arts,
Maureen with her stretches, at first were really wretched,
Paul with his technique, some sure thought they'd freak,
The way Ruth rubbed my back, she should have got a plaque
And Laura with her work, it helped relax the nerves.
The kitchen crew was great, three squares a day we ate,
There's something you should know, before we have to go,
You surely helped us all, to stand instead of fall.

"Meet you in the empty chair."

13

The Future of Psychotherapy In Addiction Treatment

The folks who come up here, come from far and near,
They come out to this place, to run their special race,
And look for a fresh start, while searching through their heart,
To each I feel so near, I hope that this is clear.

Once while I was there, I talked to empty chairs,
Feelings from the past, to live they couldn't last,
I tried to keep them in, as if it were a sin,
To cry and kick and shout, it helped to let them out,
Golf balls in my mind, they helped relieve the grind,
Colors in my brain, they helped define the pain.

Enough of all these words, I hope it's not absurd,
In closing I shall say, before we go our ways,
You helped me get in touch, with one who meant so much,
It happens to be me, a chance to be so free
Of all the pain and sorrow, that hampered my tomorrow.

(Anonymous Group Therapy Participant)

It was the early 1980s when Richard Miller brought his psychotherapeutic approach into addiction treatment. Many traditionalists

struggled with and even refuted the notion that psychotherapy could be valuable in addiction treatment. Opponents argued that psychotherapy was too general, that addicted people needed more specific treatment. Dr. Miller responded by demonstrating that psychotherapy could be tailored or directed to meet the needs of its recipients, that it could be addiction-focused. But he also made it clear that psychotherapy was essential in addiction treatment. Addictions do not arise spontaneously. Addictions, as do many mental and physical maladies, have emotional precursors. Addictions often grow out of addicted, co-dependent, abusing, confusing, unloving, and other family situations. Sometimes addictions grow out of experimental drug use, peer pressure, competitive working conditions, or spiritual malaise. Whatever the combination of precursors, and no matter how subtle they may be, there is value in emotional work on them.

Even if the rare addicted individual were to arrive in therapy with no precursors, absolutely no problems prior to addiction, with a so-called "spontaneous addiction," he or she would need a great deal of help coming out of the active phase of the addiction and adjusting to life without drugs. When people go clean or sober or get off whatever they have been overusing, they are confronted with a host of new or previously smothered feelings and a set of overwhelming challenges. Friends, enemies, family members, bosses, bill collectors (including drug dealers), and, sometimes, even the police, are waiting to greet the recovering person with reports, complaints, bills, arrests, and reprisals for behavior taking place during the addictive frenzy. All too often, waking up from the nightmare of addiction feels like going from one bad dream into another. Psychotherapy is an essential force in creating a timely and lasting outcome of addiction treatment.

Once patients have begun recovery, there are the new and massive challenges of dealing with real life without turning back to alcohol, drugs, or whatever the objects of addiction might have been, and without responding with a new addiction (for example, going from cocaine to alcohol, or from marijuana to cigarettes, or from drugs to food). Psychotherapy becomes the vehicle for recovery maintenance.

In the early years of Dr. Miller's addiction-focused group psychotherapy, one of the sources of greatest resistance was the insurer or third-party payor who supported older, "traditional," and less effective models of addiction treatment and who looked upon psychotherapy (in this arena anyway) as needless and dangerous. Times have changed. We have a long way to go, but the emotional being is now regarded as worth treating and worth sponsoring in treatment.

This issue of worth bears scrutiny. The worth of a particular treatment (psychotherapy, chemotherapy, or any other treatment) is frequently defined in terms, not of its effectiveness, but of its *cost* effectiveness. The most powerful treatment interventions are considered those that result in the greatest impact in the least amount of time at least cost to the payor (which is usually the insurance company). This is, of course, a valuable and noble approach to health and mental health care, especially in an environment of skyrocketing treatment costs. However, the determination of greatest impact or most positive outcome is, in most cases, unsophisticated and time limited. Even when seemingly sophisticated, elaborate measurements and statistical methodologies are employed in outcome measurement, analysts may be unable to determine the true or full impact of a treatment. And when that treatment is psychotherapy, outcome measurement can, at best, be a still frame excerpted from a rapidly moving and very blurry movie. The effects of even short-term psychotherapy may persist over a long period of time, or may be strongest at a date well into the future, far past the time of any outcome measurement.

Psychotherapy must also be assessed in terms of prevention. What does deep emotional work, aimed at personal insight and emotional clearing, prevent? This is a difficult question to answer, even for trained researchers. A control group (one that has never had psychotherapy) does not really offer a sound comparison to a group of those who have. Matching "control" and "experimental" individuals for precise life experiences, social support, emotional make-ups, and presenting problems is difficult. In fact, it would be foolhardy of anyone to say that any such a match was more than superficial. Add to this general difficulty in matching control and experimental individuals the problem of matching addictive patterns, behaviors, and histories, and you have a tangled web of human characteristics to study, no two of which are the same. This may be one of the reasons that psychotherapy has been viewed as relatively inessential or ineffective in addiction treatment. Its effects are difficult to study in a scientific manner.

Beyond these difficulties of evaluation is the much-denied truth that psychotherapy is not uniform in style or quality. Certainly, we would not benefit by driving all psychotherapy across the country and around the world toward uniformity in style; however, variations in the basic quality of psychotherapy are extreme, and the low end of the quality continuum is deplorable. Vulnerable, hurting people sometimes find themselves in the hands of poorly trained and even negligent psychotherapists. They remain in these hands because they do not know better, because they are afraid to quit, or because they think that they are the problem in their therapy, not the therapists.

I believe that it is essential that psychotherapists take a strong stand in favor of the use and funding of psychotherapy, especially gestalt therapy, at all levels of health and mental health care. But, this strong stand must be accompanied by another that demands quality, or responsibility for quality, among psychotherapists. Dr. Miller has led the way in applying psychotherapy to addiction treatment. He has set a high standard for quality and responsibility for himself and his staff. He has also modeled the application of general techniques, (i.e., gestalt techniques) and teachings (i.e., health instruction) to a specific area—addiction treatment. In so doing, he has created a future and a demand for psychotherapy in addiction treatment.

The next steps are just as critical as these first ones. Training in this area, which Dr. Miller has begun, must continue. Ongoing evaluation of the quality of psychotherapeutic work in addiction treatment is also a must. Continuing advocacy for third-party coverage of long-term psychotherapy in addiction and other health treatment is essential.